ENGLISH COUNTRY COOKING

ENGLISH COUNTRY COOKING

Classic Recipes From England's Homes and Pubs

CHRISTOPHER HORAN

3 9075 00023 2725

C.04

ST. MARTIN'S PRESS
NEW YORK

ENGLISH COUNTRY COOKING. Copyright © 1985 by Christopher Horan. All rights reserved. Printed in the United States of America. No part of this book may be used or reproduced in any manner whatsoever without written permission except in the case of brief quotations embodied in critical articles or reviews. For information, address St. Martin's Press, 175 Fifth Avenue, New York, N.Y. 10010.

Design by Janet Tingey

Maps by Lisa T. Davis

Library of Congress Cataloging in Publication Data

Horan, Christopher.
 English country cooking.

 1. Cookery, English. I. Title.
TX717.H718   1985   641.5942   85-1771
ISBN 0-312-25413-X

First Edition

10 9 8 7 6 5 4 3 2 1

CONTENTS

Acknowledgments viii
Using This Cookbook ix
Introduction xi
How Do Recipes Develop? xiv
Four Versions of Queen Mab's Pudding xv

ABOUT COOKING
When Is It Cooked? 2
Pressure Cooking 3
Eggs 4

LONDON
Eggs Mayonnaise 12
Chicken Liver Pâté 14
Pea and Ham Soup 16
Hot (Spicy) Indian Beef Curry 18
Cheese Poverty Soufflé 22
Jean's Lemon Middle 24
Chelsea Buns 26

THE MIDLANDS
Rarebit Cheddar Melts 35
Savory Chicken Pancakes 36
Vegetarian Shepherd's Pie 39
Cheese and Onion Pie 41
Lemon Surprise Pudding 44
Syllabub 45

THE HOME COUNTIES
Cream of Watercress Soup 51
Jerusalem Artichoke Soup 52
Honeydew Melon With Ginger 54
Christopher's Veal 55
Duckling Wizard 57
Whiskey Cream Pie 60
Sherry Trifle 62

THE NORTH OF ENGLAND
Leek and Potato Soup 70
Ham and Asparagus Rolls 72
Scotch Eggs 74
Meat and Potato Pie 76
Fish and Chips 79
Tuna Noodle Doodle 82
Bakewell Tart 83
Shortbread With Cumberland Rum Butter 85
Yorkshire Dessert 87
Rice Pudding 88

THE SOUTH OF ENGLAND
Baked Eggs 97
Roast of Chicken 98
Cauliflower, Cheese, and Bacon 102
English Fish Casserole 104
Chocolate Roll Mousse 107
Bread and Butter Pudding 110
Gingernut Biscuits 111
Irish Coffee 113

THE WEST COUNTRY
Cock-a-leekie Soup 120
My Aunt Occie's Green Tomato Chutney 122
Ploughman's Platter 124
Cornish Pasties 126
Chilton Polden Pie 128
Cream Teas 132
Apple Snow 135
Penelope Pitt's Ginger Beer 136

ACKNOWLEDGMENTS

MY THANKS TO:
Ward Lock Limited, London, for their permission to print "Queen Mab's Pudding" from their 1920s and 1980s editions of *Mrs. Beeton's Cookery and Household Management,* and "Labour-saving Apparatus" from their 1920s edition.

The British Tourist Authority in New York—particularly Mr. Bedford Pace—for photographic assistance.

My special thanks go to those who have given me encouragement over the years, especially:

Cletus and Steve Hudson, Peter Sudarsky, Linda and Ed Burke, Bonnie Mengel, Laura Sudarsky, Jenny Petersen, Mary Towner, Anna Nurse, my mother and father, Roberta Kyle, Helen and Graham Cox, Sue Cox, Leslie Perowne, Bea and Paul Cullinan, Bill and Lillian Marsano, Christiane Adler, Betty Saunders, Dorothy Hindley, Ross Hindley, James Ellinger, all my students, Ann Newman, Ruth Morrison, Sue Perkins, Barbie Crawley, Sheila Bond, Betty Saunders, my long-suffering agents Fifi Oscard and Ivy Fischer Stone and my editors Toni Lopopolo and Andrew Charron, Mark Silvester, Michael Cazel, Heather Barker, Zack Hanle, Arlene Pillar, Linda Fabbri, Bob and Sarah next door, Barbara Robson, Keith Brookes, Nigel Daly, Victoria Rose, Lynn Barrett, Barbara Rankilor from the White Horse Hotel (Helmshore, Lancashire), Mike Haynes from Macy's computer store, Sarah and Simon, Elsie Evans, Jeannie Schreyeck, Elsie Collins, Maisie Corfe, Colin Brewer, "Rene" the clean, Val Rawlinson, Arlene Pillar, Richard Porter, Aimy Fisher, and in memory of Jack Parkin Hayes.

USING THIS COOKBOOK

IF YOU are about to embark on a recipe in this book or any cookbook, please do me a favor and read not only the "ingredients" part of the recipe but the whole thing from beginning to end. It's important. Recipes are quite difficult to write and sometimes it's hard to explain everything in one paragraph, so *read the whole thing* to make sure you understand each step and that you *have the correct equipment, the right ingredients,* and *the time to make* the recipe.

Accurate measurement is very important. Some recipes you become so familiar with that you can make a similar finished dish by merely estimating the ingredients, but till then measure accurately. If things turn out wrong, ask yourself, did I really measure accurately?

INTRODUCTION

THE object of this book is to outline English cooking as I know it today. All my recipes can be tackled by those new to the kitchen, and they should prepare you well for some of the dishes you might be offered should you ever decide to pay us a visit.

I expect my own countrymen will be outraged when they see what dishes I have associated with each area, but the truth is my homeland is very small by American standards and as a result the English are well traveled within their own country. It is often difficult to identify a dish with a particular area. You could as easily be offered Yorkshire pudding in Cornwall as in Yorkshire (and I doubt that it would be made any better in Yorkshire).

For some years I worked for Aer Lingus, and as part of the job used to have to travel England giving lectures about the Irish countryside. It always surprised me to learn how few British people knew that the Republic of Ireland was a separate country, even with all the publicity concerning the political strife in Northern Ireland. I have found the same is true in America, so let me clear up this confusing little problem. Great Britain (named "Great" to distinguish it from "Little Britain" or Brittany, in France) consists of four basic regions, which at one time were also separate countries. These are Scotland, Wales, Northern Ireland and England. Each has its own culture, customs, language, and eating habits. Even today the differences are easily detectable and easily seen in language. Someone from the highlands of Scotland would be as hard pressed to understand my accent as I would be to understand his.

For the purposes of this book I am confining myself to my own part of Great Britain—England—for I am an Anglo-Saxon.

No one country has a monopoly on good cooking (though I

sometimes think the French think so) and the more I learn about recipes, their country of origin and recipe technique, the more I realize that there are hundreds of basic recipes common to all.

The English diet has been mocked by foreigners for a long time but I would like to suggest to you that things have changed. Food standards both in an Englishman's home and in his restaurants are considerably higher now than they were twenty years ago.

With all the latest scientific evidence pointing to the important role diet plays in leading a healthy life, it is obvious that what we eat is important. I believe that healthy eating habits are the most important thing of all. Training our young to get into the habit of eating regular, balanced meals is one of the best lessons we can teach them, far better than training them to take their daily vitamin pills. If you learn what foods contain what vitamins, you can adjust your diet properly. For example, in the winter it's healthy to get into the habit of eating at least one piece of fruit a day. All year round include in your daily diet enough roughage food to keep your system healthy (that is, celery, many green vegetables, cereals, and the like). Your body and digestive system is designed *precisely* to accept food in its natural form; pills are not what the average human stomach expects. You can get an excellent publication from the government called *Nutritive Value of Foods* free by writing to: United States Department of Agriculture, Human Nutrition Information Service, Consumer Nutrition Center, 6505 Belcrest Road, Hyattsville, Maryland 20782.

It also occurs to me that we all get too caught up with food advertising and fall victims to the power of the media, who thrive on encouraging us to follow the latest food fads so that their latest new "low-cal" product will sell—"low-cal" often being a euphemism for even less nutrition in a mass-produced product.

The best way of beating the food fad system is to prepare more meals from scratch at home; then you can *be sure* what you're eating. Many of my dishes are inexpensive to make and easy to follow.

If you're one of those whose heart sinks every time you enter the kitchen at the thought of having to produce yet another meal,

I sympathize. I am a working person with a full-time career, I'm renovating the home I live in, and I have to entertain a lot. There's always chaos everywhere. I have, like many of you, very little time. However, occasionally I use cooking as a method of relaxation. Ahead of time I start hoarding ingredients with the thought in the back of my mind that I might possibly cook at the weekend. I wear comfortable clothes and play music and tackle dishes that I don't have time to prepare during the week. Don't be scared to try something new . . . even if it happens to be English.

If you try any of these dishes, I hope you'll be rewarded by an excellent result. Sometimes recipes don't work because there's a mistake in the actual recipe, or it's so badly worded that it's difficult to figure out what you're supposed to do. I try to tell you what I actually do, rather than what is the conventional method.

Finally, a word for those who are starting out in the kitchen for the first time. If your early results aren't an instant success, keep going—you need to practice before you find the best way of doing things. I have ruined hundreds of dishes to gain my experience, have cut my fingers innumerable times . . . and still do. It's one thing to do nothing else other than follow a recipe, but quite another to weave cooking in with the hectic pace of life in the 1980s.

Happy cooking.

HOW DO RECIPES DEVELOP?

I HAVE inherited a real treasure from the past. My father recently discovered a small, rather insignificant, hand-written book lurking in some dark area of his attic as he was sifting through junk trying to find something. On closer inspection this odd exercise book with very old-fashioned writing appeared to be some kind of recipe book. On even closer inspection and with much hard work, my father discovered that the original owner of the little book was my great-great-grandmother, Baroness de Fobeck! Indeed it is a collection of recipes she gathered from friends and newspaper articles.

It makes very interesting reading, as it gives a sideways view of English household conditions in the mid to late nineteenth century. Most of the recipes are very approximate and lack accuracy. There is no mention of temperatures, other than comments like "Place on a hot fire." (An iron range fueled by coal would have been used, in which there was a primitive and rather unreliable oven.) Many of the ingredients specified are now known by other names or have been replaced altogether.

I have tried a couple of the recipes—mostly with very uninteresting results (English cooking has *definitely* improved) but as I started to work through the book I came upon an English recipe for a dessert that is still popular today, Queen Mab's Pudding. I then followed the recipe through the works of Mrs. Beeton. Here are three original versions of the same recipe—and mine to complete the picture—a century of Queen Mab's Puddings!

Four Versions of QUEEN MAB'S PUDDING

An extract from my great-great-grandmother's private recipe book. Queen Mab's Pudding, a recipe she acquired from Mrs. Brown in 1873.

QUEEN MAB'S PUDDING
(Translation)

as taken from my great-great-grandmother, the Baroness de Fobeck, dated 1873, and taken from her friend Mrs. Brown

¾ of an ounce isinglass° in one pint of new milk, 8 bitter and 8 sweet almonds, the peel of a large lemon, a small piece of vanilla, 4½ ounces of white sugar, 1 pint of good cream thickened as a custard with the yolks of 6 fresh eggs; when nearly cold, add to the milk and isinglass, the custard; continue to stir it until quite cold, then lay any dried fruits you may have in a pattern in your mold, and mix 2 ounces of dried cherries, 2 ounces of candied orange and citron peel and dried preserved ginger or any other dried desert fruits you may like to use up.

° Isinglass was used as a substitute for gelatine.

Four Versions of Queen Mab's Pudding

QUEEN MAB'S PUDDING

as printed in the 1920s edition of
Mrs. Beeton's Guide to Cookery and Household Management

minutes. Melt the gelatine in 1 tablespoonful of water, and mix with the contents of the stewpan, add a few drops of cochineal, and turn into a large mould rinsed with cold water.

TIME.—About 1 hour. SUFFICIENT for 4 or 5 persons.

QUEEN MAB'S PUDDING.

INGREDIENTS.—3 oz. of castor sugar, 1 oz. of gelatine, 1 pint of milk, ¼ of a pint of double cream, 3 eggs, 2 oz. of glacé cherries halved, 1 oz. of candied citron peel shredded, vanilla essence.

478   MRS. BEETON'

METHOD.—Soak the gelatine in the milk for ½ an hour, then stir it over the fire until dissolved, and add the sugar. Cool slightly, put in the yolks of eggs and cream, stir by the fire until the mixture thickens, but it must not boil. Let it cool, add the cherries, citron and vanilla to taste, stir until on the point of setting, then turn into a mould previously lined with jelly, or rinsed with cold water.

TIME.—About 1 hour. SUFFICIENT for 5 or 6 persons.

An extract from the 1920s version of Mrs. Beeton's Cookery and Household Management, *Queen Mab's Pudding.*

QUEEN MAB'S PUDDING

as printed in the 1980s edition of
*Mrs. Beeton's Guide to Cookery and
Household Management*

Queen Mab's Pudding

4 helpings

oil for greasing
400ml milk
pared rind of 1 lemon
3 eggs
75g caster sugar
a few drops almond essence

4 × 15ml spoons water
1 × 10ml spoon gelatine
50g glacé cherries
25g cut mixed peel or whole citron peel
125ml double cream

Decoration (optional)
whipped cream   glacé cherries

Oil a 750ml mould lightly. Warm the milk with the lemon rind, but do not let it boil. Mix the eggs and sugar together until fluffy and pale, and slowly stir in the milk. Strain the custard back into the pan or into a double boiler or basin held over hot water. (Make sure the water does not touch the upper pan.) Cook over very low heat for 15–20 minutes, stirring all the time, until it thickens. Do not let it come near the boil. Strain the custard into a bowl, stir in the almond essence, and leave to cool.

Put the water into a heatproof container, sprinkle in the gelatine and leave to soften. Stand the container in a pan of hot water and stir until the gelatine dissolves. Cool slightly and add to the custard. Leave in a cool place until it begins to set, stirring from time to time to prevent a skin forming.

Halve the cherries and chop the peel finely. Stir the fruit into the setting custard. Whip the cream until it is semi-stiff and fold in. Pour the pudding into the prepared mould and leave to set for about 2 hours. Turn out on to a flat, wetted plate.

Alternatively, pour the pudding into individual glasses, leave to set for about 1 hour and decorate with whipped cream and glacé cherries.

The 1980s version of Queen Mab's Pudding as found in Mrs. Beeton's Cookery and Household Management.

QUEEN MAB'S DESSERT

by Christopher Horan — 1985

6 servings
Preparation time: 40 minutes
Cooling time: approximately 2 hours

Queen Mab is a mystical figure whose main claim to fame is the part she plays in Shakespeare's *Romeo and Juliet* (Act 1, Scene IV). Mercutio is explaining to his friend, Romeo, that he has dreamed that dreamers often lie.

> ROMEO: In bed asleep while they do dream things true.
> MERCUTIO: O! then, I see, Queen Mab hath been with you.
> She is the fairies' midwife, and she comes
> In shape no bigger than an agate stone
> On the forefinger of an alderman,
> Drawn with a team of little atomies
> Athwart men's noses as they lie asleep.
> . . . she gallops night by night
> . . . O'er ladies' lips, who straight on kisses dream . . .

What an appropriate name, therefore, for a lovely old English cold dessert. Let us pretend that the almonds are agate stones, and that the custard is light enough to pass any fine lady's lips!

Special equipment needed: a 2-pint mold or 6 stemmed wine glasses, medium-sized metal mixing bowl, hand electric mixer or balloon whisk, pastry brush, wax paper, small heavy-bottomed pan, thermometer, wooden spoon, a large 4-quart pan or double boiler.

3 medium-sized fresh eggs at room temperature
½ cup *(3½ ounces)* superfine sugar
2 cups *(16 fluid ounces)* fresh milk
A small piece of lemon rind
2 *(1½)* level teaspoons powdered gelatine
4 *(3)* tablespoons of water
¼ cup *(1 ounce)* candied peel
Just under ½ cup *(2 ounces)* candied cherries
½ cup *(4 fluid ounces)* heavy cream, lightly whipped
DECORATION
½ pint *(8 fluid ounces)* heavy cream, whipped
Candied cherries
10 whole peeled almonds

METHOD: Carefully grease a 2-pint mold with a pastry brush, making sure you reach all parts of the mold. In a medium-sized metal bowl using a hand electric mixer or a balloon whisk, beat the eggs and sugar till they turn pale and the grittiness of the sugar disappears.

In a small pan warm the milk and lemon rind, but do not boil it. At the same time put a 4-quart pan containing about 2 inches of water on to boil. When the milk is warm, remove the rind, then whisk the milk into the egg and sugar mixture and place the bowl over the pan of barely simmering water (alternatively, you can turn the mixture into a double boiler, if you have one). Stir occasionally, and after 15 minutes the mixture will start to thicken slightly. Do not leave the cooking range during these 15 minutes; it's important that the custard doesn't boil or break down—the water in the pan should not touch the bowl at all. If you use a thermometer, the custard is done when its temperature reaches 180° F.

In a small, thick-bottomed saucepan sprinkle the gelatine onto the 4 *(3)* tablespoons water and heat very gently until the gelatine has dissolved; this won't take long. Allow to cool for a few minutes and add to the custard. Stir in the candied peel, cherries, and lightly whipped cream, and place on the custard a piece of wax paper that completely covers the custard's surface. Leave to cool for half an hour.

When the custard has cooled to hand hot pour it into the prepared mold, and when completely cool refrigerate it for two hours. If you don't own a pretty china or metal mold, then divide the mixture into stem wine glasses; individual desserts always look attractive.

To remove the dessert from the mold, fill your sink with the hottest water you can get from your faucet and lower the mold into the hot water, being careful that no water gets onto the surface of the dessert. Hold it there for about 10 to 15 seconds, then place your serving dish upside down over the top of the mold and in one swift movement up-end the whole lot so that the mold is sitting on the plate decorative side up. Sometimes the contents will be very stubborn and will remain in the mold. If this happens leave the dessert as is for a few minutes; gravity will usually do the rest.

Finally, decorate with whipped cream, candied cherries and almonds, and store in the refrigerator until needed. You can prepare the dessert ahead of time but it should not be taken out of the mold more than two hours before serving.

ABOUT COOKING

WHEN IS IT COOKED?

IN LEARNING to cook, one of the main problems is to know "When is it cooked?"

In writing a recipe, you give cooking times based on your own experience (and other people's) and the conditions that surround your own kitchen—the time of year (and therefore the room humidity and temperature), your measuring equipment, the calibration of your oven, whether you cook on gas or electricity or bottled gas, and so on. It's often difficult to give precise instructions, as the conditions in your kitchen may easily be different from mine.

One way to tell whether it's done or not is: Does it smell cooked? You may find this an odd comment; often when you start smelling it it's too late—it's burnt. But my point is use your God-given gifts, one being smell. If you set something in the oven to cook, tell your smell "buds" to wake up and tell you when it smells ready; you'll be surprised by the results! Use your sixth sense to guide you as to whether to take it out straightaway or leave it in a little longer.

If you want an example of this I'll explain. Some people walk around their apartment or house with a kitchen timer—they have it about their person while they're watching TV or chatting to a neighbor on the stoop. Then when it goes off they go and check on their morning's work. I'm not organized enough to do that. And as I'm sitting here writing this, I have two Cornish game hens roasting in the oven. My writing room is about thirty yards from my kitchen, and when the smell of cooked chicken reaches my room I know from experience that it's time to remove them from the oven—they're done! So excuse me a few moments while I go and investigate.

PRESSURE COOKING

IN THE United States, the pressure cooker is considered to be rather passé. Instead we are offered ranges with built-in microwaves. No thanks!

When the microwave oven was first introduced in England there were many skeptics who said that food eaten out of a microwave would give you cancer. Quite obviously that's stupid. A microwave heats by electronically causing friction between the two molecules of hydrogen and one molecule of oxygen that make up a particle of water. Therefore, it will only heat foods with water in them. If you place a china plate of flour in a microwave nothing much will happen. Their biggest advantage is in the defrosting process.

Did you know that a pressure cooker costing much, much less will do just as efficient a job of defrosting? It will also do a lot more besides.

Pressure cookers are excellent for speeding up lengthy cooking periods for cheaper cuts of meat. In twenty minutes you can cook to dropping point two pounds of shin beef that would normally take three hours in a low oven. A microwave won't do that nearly as satisfactorily.

If a recipe calls for a lengthy steaming time—for example, a plum pudding—you can rapidly accelerate the cooking time by using a pressure cooker. The Presto Company makes the best, in my opinion. Not only is the pot solid, I like the pressure mechanism and find the instruction booklet very clear and helpful. I take my pressure cooker everywhere I go—even camping. Especially camping. It also doubles as an excellent heavy-bottomed saucepan.

EGGS

AN EGG is a very important ingredient in cooking—many of these recipes and ones you'll find in other cookbooks use eggs. A recipe won't work properly if the egg isn't fresh and at room temperature. I therefore do not think it is a good idea to keep eggs in a refrigerator. Most Americans walk into my kitchen and gasp in horror at the small basket of eggs I keep on the counter.

So then, how can you tell if an egg is fresh? First you always need to check the date stamp on the box, and make sure you buy a box that's within the expiration date stamped on the side. However, this means little.

The acid test is by cracking one open onto a plate and observing what you see. The yolk should be firm, yellowy, and have a nice thick membrane covering it. Surrounding the yolk should be a firm part of white, translucent, and surrounding that a less firm part. If the two distinctions of the white are not clearly defined then the egg is not fresh, or to put it another way, if the egg white is watery and spreads itself over the whole plate it's not fresh. If you live in an area where the climate is such that you have to keep your eggs in the refrigerator, then be sure to remove to room temperature the number you'll need at least one hour beforehand. When my instructions say "2 fresh eggs at room temperature" I mean what I say.

LONDON

A view looking up Piccadilly as seen from Piccadilly Circus. Photo taken in the late 1950s.

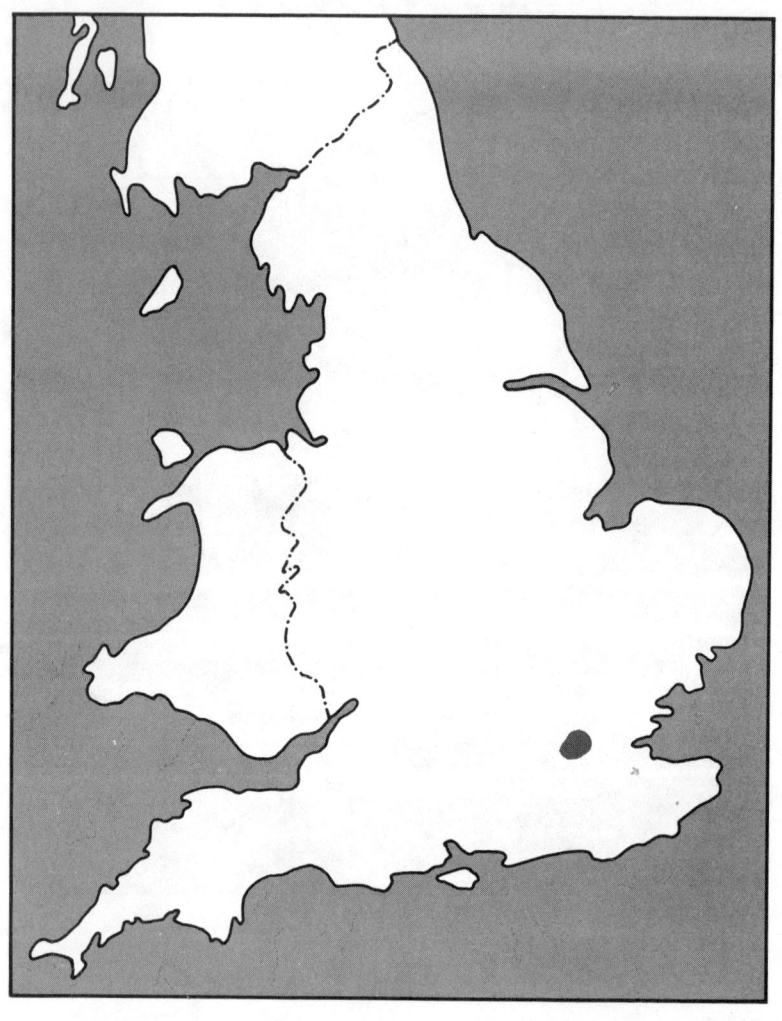

IF YOU'VE ever been to England, you've been to London. Nearly all flights from America land in London. Many Americans' experience of British food is the food they eat either at Heathrow or in their London hotel—no wonder Americans have a low opinion of English food.

In many cities the best places to eat are not in the most accessible places, you have to search them out; London is no exception. The large food chains do not provide the most authentic food or the most delicious, so don't judge the food in England by the meals you eat in your hotel. Be adventurous, eat out—but be careful. London was never built with foreigners in mind. You won't find a nice neat grid system of streets and avenues as in many American cities. Roads go at all angles and no amount of logic will get you around. I have lived in London nearly all my life and still get lost. You absolutely *have* to get hold of an "A to Z" map book of London. Having an "underground" guide isn't enough in itself—you might want to get to an address on, say, the Cromwell road, and yet the nearest subway stop will be called "South Kensington."

The best places to eat lunch are the great pubs of London. You choose your pub very carefully. There is a very good publication called *The Good Pub Guide,* published by the same people who publish the English equivalent of *Consumer Reports* (known as *Which?*). It's a paperback and covers the whole of the United Kingdom. When choosing a pub for lunch there are a few things to remember. Like it or not, the English one-upmanship is based on class, not necessarily money—and rather like bars in the States, each pub caters to a specialized clientele. That's one of the reasons you'll often find a number of pubs in close proximity to each other. You'll have to do bit of investigating to decide which is the pub for you.

Many of our pubs (public houses) are very old, and some are not. I find it rather sad that many breweries are ripping down the interiors to make way for the modern look. In Victorian times a pub would often consist of several different bars. The "public" bar would be for the "riffraff," or the manual worker who didn't want to dress up, and the "lounge" (or "snug") would be for a more genteel clientele. Although the current fad is to create one very large bar for ease of running, you'll still find this division, if you seek it out. You'll also notice that the prices are slightly cheaper in the public bars.

Pubs also cater to professions. In the City of London you will notice that many of the pubs are filled with official-looking people—attorneys (known as solicitors), magistrates, clerks, and so on; in Fleet Street you'll find editors and other publishing types. Most people will go to their local pub at either lunchtime or after work, so when you enter a pub, don't go only for the food and drink, go also to look at the people.

It's quite acceptable for women to enter lounge areas of our pubs unaccompanied, and although women might be reluctant to do so in many American bars, you can do it quite safely in England. Most women order half-pints of beer, not pints (though I can't imagine why). However, when in Rome . . .

It might be helpful for you to know a couple of things about the English law concerning pubs. Most pub hours are 10:30 A.M. till 3:00 P.M., then open again at 5:30 P.M. till 10:30 P.M. On Fridays and Saturdays many pubs can stay open till 11:00 P.M. Hours vary slightly depending on the county (the English equivalent to state) so you'll need to be aware of the hours applicable to each county. When I was a teenager I used to go to a pub in Hertfordshire that would close at 10:30 P.M., have a pint there, and then belt across the county border to Middlesex, where closing time was half an hour later.

It's a tradition that five or ten minutes before closing the bartender or landlord will yell, "Your last orders please, ladies and gentlemen." This is your sign that the joint is going to close. Then they will announce, "Time, gentlemen, *please.*" This means drink up and get out. I once worked for a wonderful Cockney landlady who used to yell, "Ladies and gentlemen! Give us your glasses and show us your asses," which in Britain is quite rude—but because people liked her she got away with it.

There is one more tidbit you might be interested in and that's inns. Inns are slightly different from pubs—legally speaking, that is. There is an old English law still on the statute books that no government has had time to reform, and that is that any pub known as an "inn" cannot refuse a traveler food, refreshment, or accommodation. It dates back to the times when inns were coaching inns—a network of stopping places for coaches pulled by a team of horses. At the inn there would be a change of horses.

Today, theoretically, you could present yourself at an inn and demand accommodation. Most landlords would look at you as if you had a screw loose, as they are not aware of this little legal quirk, so I don't recommend that you try it!

Nowhere else in the country is there a higher concentration of pubs than in London. A pub can often be the center of social activity of a neighborhood. You should not enter a pub unless you know what kind of beverages you can order. Beers in England differ dramatically from the beers you're used to. Don't prejudge them; many are very good. Much of the beer drunk in the United States is chemically produced, and indeed England has its fair share of this kind of beer. You can usually distinguish it easily, as it has a commercial name and is cooled. A real beer is a live beer (that means that the chemical reaction that is activated by brewing hops and adding yeast and sugar is still going on). A live beer will not live if it's cooled for a long period and this is one of the reasons you find the English drinking "warm beer." For a start, it's much more tasty.

Each brewery's beer has slight differences. There are many local breweries that supply quite a small area, and most breweries produce a "bitter" beer and "mild" beer. I always used to laugh when Americans walked into a bar where I was working and says "A pint of bitters"—it used to sound funny.

You will discover many kinds of beers that you can't find in the

States and many odd local names for various combinations. The best one I can think of to recommend to you is shandy. If you don't usually drink beer try a pint of shandy; you won't regret it—especially on a hot day. It's a mix of half bitter beer on draught (tap) and half lemonade (or 7-Up) or fizzy ginger beer. I prefer the ginger beer version—more flavor, very thirst quenching. You see many barmen struggling with the froth that forms when the beer hits the lemonade. The correct way of making a shandy is to put the lemonade in first, then add the beer.

Here are a few more local terms that I've collected that you might find amusing and helpful:

Snowball: a mixture of advocaat (a liqueur made from egg yolks and brandy) mixed with lime juice and 7-Up

A pint of mild and bitter: half a pint of bitter and half of mild, on tap

Stout ale: a dark beer made from roasted hops and brown sugar

A pint of mother-in-law: Half a pint of stout and half of bitter(!)

Black and tan: a half of bitter, a half of Guinness

A barley wine: a very strong beer made from barley—rather sweet

Rum and black: dark rum served with black-currant juice (like blueberry)

Snakebite: half a pint of bitter and half of real alcoholic "cider"

Cider: not the same as American—it's fermented and very good

Banana split: a half of bitter with a half of lager

Bitter top: a pint of bitter with an inch of 7-Up on the top

Black velvet: half a pint of Guinness, half a pint of cider

Hot toddy: a shot (measure) of Scotch, sugar, lemon juice, and hot water

You will also notice that in many places people ask for "crisps"—these are potato chips. "Pork scratchings" are made from the skin of pigs; very crispy and delicious, good with beer. There are many more terms but this will give you a start.

Food in London today is very cosmopolitan, and you will find good examples of the world's many cuisines available there. And like everywhere else, paying a high price for a meal doesn't necessarily guarantee good food or service. The English are notoriously bad at providing good service, and London is no exception. I find I have to "humor" serving staff into giving me good service. You'll discover the best way of doing this, but flashing wads of money and demanding service won't do much good, I'm afraid.

It's an odd thing, but if you travel to New York, for example, you'll find some of the best Chinese food in the world. The same is true of London with Indian food. If you've never had an Indian meal before, I *urge* you to do so. Try a curry with all the accompaniments, but be careful—this is very hot, spicy food, and it can blow the roof of your mouth off! Best to order it "mild" to start with. My recipe for curry will give you an insight into what you can expect.

The English will invite complete strangers into their homes—we love having visitors, especially Americans. If you start chatting to someone on the street and they end up by inviting you home, go! For in our homes you'll get a real opportunity to eat "English."

One final word about London. The subway system stops at about midnight, though the bus systems go, for the most part, through the night; the routes they take, however, are rather difficult to fathom. Getting a taxi after midnight can also be like looking for a needle in a haystack. London does not run 24 hours a day like many American cities, and as London is so spread out (rather than built high), this can be a problem. You'll find your stay much less traumatic if you start your evening foray into London's delights earlier in the evening and head home earlier.

EGGS MAYONNAISE

4 servings
Preparation time: 30 minutes

This is an appetizer I've not seen served in America at all. It's so easy a child could do it. I like it because I've usually got the ingredients, and sometimes when I've forgotten to plan a starter I can do it as an afterthought (though I don't tell the guests that — it's always good PR to let them think you've been slaving over a hot stove for at least the week).

Special equipment needed: a large mixing bowl, a 2-quart saucepan with a lid, a large balloon whisk or a hand electric mixer, four nice 6-inch *(15-centimeter)* glass serving plates

4 large, fresh eggs, unshelled, at room temperature
1 fresh egg yolk at room temperature
1 cup *(8 fluid ounces)* good quality light corn oil at room temperature (I find that olive oil is too strong for this delicate cold sauce)
Juice from half a nice, juicy, fresh lemon
2 *(1½)* tablespoons cider vinegar
1 *(¾)* teaspoon dry English mustard
1 *(¾)* teaspoon sugar (preferably 'superfine')
Freshly ground white pepper and salt (optional) to taste
GARNISH
4 large lettuce leaves
1 small can anchovies

METHOD: First take the four large eggs and carefully pierce the rounded end of each egg with a little hole, so that the air can escape during cooking and the shells won't crack. Put the eggs in the pan, cover with cold water, and bring to the boil quickly. When boiling point is reached, turn off the heat, cover the pan with a tight-fitting lid, and leave for *exactly* 10 minutes. When the time is up remove the lid and run cold water over the eggs. Tap each so it cracks and put to one side.

Now make the mayonnaise. There's a lot of rubbish talked about how difficult this is to make. It's not; if I can do it you can. You just have to follow a few simple rules. All the ingredients must be at room temperature, especially the oil. In cold climates or during the winter you may find it necessary to warm the oil slightly, but don't expect the sauce to "make" if you use oil straight from the refrigerator. Also the freshness of the egg yolk is very important.

In a large mixing bowl (I use a china one) place the egg yolk. To separate the yolk from the white, firmly crack the shell on a hard surface and then, over a bowl, transfer the contents carefully from one half shell to the other until the white falls away from the yolk. Now take your balloon whisk and start working it. You'll feel a bit silly to start with as it seems as if you're whisking nothing. Don't worry; you'll be amazed at what's going to happen. Whisking all the time, slowly *drip by drip* pour on the oil. Immediately you'll notice it start to get thick. Keep whisking all the while. As the sauce forms you can add the oil more quickly. When you've poured in about two-thirds of the oil, add the lemon juice. This will help to thin it. Continue to add the remaining oil in the same way. Then add all the rest of the ingredients and whisk it. I usually leave the salt to the last as it's easy to put too much in.

Shell each hard-cooked egg, and cut each in half lengthwise. On each serving plate place a piece of lettuce large enough to cover the plate, then place on to it the two egg halves, yolk side down. Spoon enough of your homemade mayonnaise on each half egg to cover the white and place two pieces of anchovy so they cross on the top.

A tip if the sauce goes funny or "splits" while you're making it: This has happened to me many times. You're in a hurry and pour on the oil too quickly. Don't panic! Merely pour the failure into another clean bowl and thoroughly wash the whisk and mixing bowl. Then put two tablespoons of *boiling* water into the large mixing bowl and again start whisking, adding the "failure" a drip at a time. This should restore your emulsion and you can continue adding the oil and other ingredients. It works!

You can make this dish ahead of time and keep it in the refrigerator for about two hours, though you should not assemble each serving, put the mayonnaise on, or garnish until the last moment. When you're eating your portion remember to notice what a lovely change homemade mayonnaise is from manufactured. I'm sure you'll agree there is a lot of difference.

CHICKEN LIVER PÂTÉ

4 large servings
Preparation time: 30 minutes
Cooling and setting time: 12 hours

I've included this as an English starter because I see few people making pâté in the States. It's very easy to make and inexpensive. The word pâté is, of course, stolen from the French. I think the English would call it meat paste. I like to make it because liver is healthy for you and made this way it is extremely palatable. You will often find it on the menus of London restaurants, usually called chef's pâté or house pâté.

Special equipment needed: a large heavy skillet, a wooden spoon, a blender or sieve, 4 nice little presentation dishes or 1 larger serving pot (I like to use earthenware)

¾ cup *(6 ounces)* lightly salted butter
½ pound *(8 ounces)* fresh chicken livers
2 tablespoons dry sherry or brandy *(1½)*
2 teaspoons English dry mustard *(1½)*
1½ teaspoons mixed herbs *(1⅛)* (you can experiment, using your favorite herbs)
2 cloves of garlic, minced
1 small onion, finely diced
Salt and freshly ground black pepper
¼ cup *(2 ounces)* melted butter to pour over the finished dish
Parsley for decoration

METHOD: In a large, thick-bottomed saucepan melt about ¼ cup *(2 ounces)* of the ¾ cup *(6 ounces)* of butter and fry the chicken livers on a medium heat. Livers cook quickly but keep turning them with a wooden spoon, as there's nothing worse than raw liver. After 5 minutes add the remaining butter, and the remaining ingredients, and stir for a further 3 minutes.

Now stick the whole lot into the blender or food processor. If you need to add a little water to aid the blending, that's OK—but not too much or you'll end up with soup rather than a paste. If you don't own a blender or processor you can work the mixture through a sieve with a wooden spoon.

When the mixture is smooth—say 30 seconds of blending—turn out into your serving pot or dishes and pour a little melted butter over the surface of each. Then chill thoroughly for 12 hours in your refrigerator. I usually decorate each with a tiny "flower" (sprig) of fresh parsley just before serving.

In England this dish is traditionally served with "soldiers." Soldiers are made by buttering a piece of hot toast, removing the crusts, and then cutting into 3 or 4 fingers. The toast must be served hot.

PEA AND HAM SOUP

6 to 10 servings
Preparation time: 30 minutes
Cooking time: 3 hours and 15 minutes

This is not a dish you decide to make on the spur of the moment, and I wouldn't recommend that you rush out and buy the ingredients just so that you can make the soup. The decision to make it all hinges around having the bone of a baked ham—and that's not something you just go and buy. But on those occasions when you have had a joint of ham and you are wondering what to do with the bone, maybe you'll remember having flicked through this book and will use the recipe. I've included it as a London dish because we have an expression in London for a very foggy day: a "pea-souper." This really goes back to the late nineteenth century when London generated its power and heat from coal. The smoke mixed with the atmosphere in such a way that a very heavy smog (smoke and fog) would form for days on end, making any kind of journey virtually impossible. The soup is quite thick, like that pea-soup fog.

Special equipment needed: a 4-quart, heavy-bottomed saucepan or a large pressure cooker, a large mixing bowl, a blender or a sieve, a wooden spoon

2 *(1 1/2)* tablespoons corn oil
1 celery stalk, well washed and roughly chopped
1 medium onion, peeled and roughly chopped
1 large carrot, roughly chopped
Approximately 2 quarts *(64 fluid ounces)* water
1 large ham bone
2 cups *(16 ounces)* dried green split peas
2 cloves garlic, minced
2 bay leaves
4 slices lean bacon, cooked
Salt and freshly ground black pepper

METHOD: First of all you have to make stock. The word terrifies many people but it's merely the result of boiling water with bones and/or vegetables and makes all the difference to soups and stews—and definitely distinguishes bought from homemade. In your large 4-quart saucepan place the oil, celery, onion, and carrot, and "sweat" them over medium heat. This means putting a lid on the pan and shaking them over the heat for about 5 minutes so that the vegetables start to release their juices. Now add the water and bone, bring to the boil, and simmer for 2 hours. If you are using a pressure cooker, cook at the highest pressure (15 pounds per square inch) for 20 minutes.

Strain off the liquid, discard the bone and "veggies," clean the pan, and pour the liquid back into the pan.

Now add the split peas, garlic, bay leaves, and bacon. Bring to the boil and simmer gently for about 1 hour and 15 minutes till the peas are soft. Either put the whole lot through your blender or food processor or push through a sieve. Dried peas absorb quite a lot of liquid and if the soup starts to get any thicker than heavy cream, add a little water.

Add salt and freshly ground black pepper to taste and serve with croutons made by drying small pieces of bread in a low oven or quickly frying them in light oil.

HOT (SPICY) INDIAN BEEF CURRY with accompaniments

3 servings
Preparation time: 45 minutes
Cooking time: 1 hour (depending on the quality of meat)

London is full of good Indian restaurants, usually run by Indians. Indian food has been part of the English diet for well over a century, going back to the time when many British families were stationed in India during the British protectorate. (If you saw the BBC TV series "Jewel in the Crown," you'll understand.) As a result of the Commonwealth immigration rules, many Indians are entitled to a British passport and are therefore permitted to live in England. Their curries are quite delicious, but you will need to develop a taste for a mild curry before your palate becomes adjusted to the heat of a curry that an Indian would eat. Curries are eaten in hot climates to induce "a real good sweat," which in turn activates the body's natural cooling system; so although it may seem illogical to eat very hot (spicy) food in hot weather, there is a good reason for it. One more word on curry. A real curry is made from a number of spices; each spice subtly changes the flavor. In England, with the increased availability of such spices as coriander seeds, cumin seeds, turmeric, and cardamom, the English, like the Indians, are in the habit of grinding their own curry powder. This recipe, using bought powder, will serve to give you a taste of what is in store for you if you eat Indian food in London. (By the way, in my opinion there is a great difference between curry powder you buy in a supermarket from the spice rack and freshly imported powder you buy from a specialty store. If you get the opportunity to buy good powder, do it and store it in a very well-sealed jar, removing as much air as possible. You never know how long these spices in supermarkets have been hanging around, losing all their flavor.)

Special equipment needed: a 4-quart, flameproof casserole dish with lid (preferably an oven-to-table type), a wooden spoon, three nice side serving dishes, a sieve or colander with thin holes, tongs, paper towels, a teakettle

3 tablespoons light corn oil
1 pound good-quality steak (sirloin, chuck, or London broil) *(2¼)*
2 medium onions, peeled and diced
4 heaped teaspoons good-quality, *freshly purchased* curry powder *(3)*
1 cubic inch fresh ginger, cut into tiny pieces *(2½ cubic centimeters)* (you may use a teaspoon of powdered ginger if you can't get fresh)
1 piece of thinly peeled lemon rind
2 cloves of garlic, peeled and minced
1 pint *(16 fluid ounces) (2¼)* water
1 green apple, peeled, cored, and chopped into ¼-inch *(¾-centimeter)* cubes
3 tablespoons red raisins

ACCOMPANIMENTS
1 cup *(5⅓ ounces)* dry-roasted peanuts
1 small jar Green Tomato Chutney *(see page 122)* or lime pickle
1 carton natural yogurt, 8-ounce
1 small cucumber, pealed and diced, *or* 1 banana, sliced
3 pints, water *(48 fluid ounces)*
½ teaspoon *(large pinch)* salt
2 *(1½)* tablespoons of olive oil
1½ cups *(11⅔ ounces)* unbleached long-grain white rice
At hand 1½ more pints *(24 fluid ounces)* boiling water
1 nice juicy lemon, cut into wedges
6 popadams *(see note)*
Oil for deep-frying popadams

METHOD: Now then, just because there's a lot of writing to this recipe doesn't mean it's difficult. Just follow each step carefully. First, place your flameproof casserole on top of the stove on a medium heat and add the oil. As the oil is heating up cut the meat into cubes, removing any excess fat; then add meat to the oil. Brown and seal the meat by cooking it briskly for 10 minutes, turning it occasionally with a wooden spoon. If some of the meat sticks to the bottom at first, don't worry; it will free itself after a few minutes of cooking. Now add the onions and cook for a further 5 minutes, stirring occasionally.

Now add the curry powder. Four (3) heaped teaspoons will produce a medium strength curry, 2 (1½) will give a mild one, and 6 (4) will blow your head off. You will have to decide the quantity, which will partially be determined by your guests.

Now add the ginger, the lemon rind, and garlic, and stir in one pint *(16 fluid ounces)* water. Cover and barely simmer for one hour if you are using a high-quality steak; allow more time if you are using a less expensive cut. When the meat is tender you can either complete the dish or cool, cover, and refrigerate. It will keep for three days.

To complete the dish you must prepare the rice and the side dishes. This takes me about half an hour. It tends to be rather a crazy half-hour so be prepared for some fast work, as the timing is important — everything has to come together at more or less the same time.

In the three little side dishes (I use pretty little rice bowls) place the peanuts, the chutney, and the yogurt. Into the yogurt stir the cucumber, diced into ½-inch *(1¼-centimeter)* cubes. In hot weather chill the yogurt and cucumber. If you prefer, you can add a peeled and sliced banana to the yogurt instead of the cucumber.

Now gently heat the curry. You may need to adjust the consistency, which needs to be like a medium-thick gravy. If the juice is too runny, allow it to reduce by gently boiling, uncovered, so some of the liquid evaporates. If it is too thick, add a little water — often refrigerating dries a dish out. About 10 minutes before you're ready to serve add the apple cubes and raisins.

The main accompaniment is the rice, and here you will have excellent results every time if you follow my rules. In a 4-quart saucepan bring one pint *(16 fluid ounces)* per person of water to boil and add the salt and oil. At the *same* time bring about half that quantity of extra water to boil in a teakettle. Add ½ cup *(3⁷/₈ ounces)* of rice per person (huge appetites will manage a cup per person) to the first pan and cook for 7 minutes. (As you increase the amounts, the cooking time gets a little shorter.) I break all conventional rules and stir the rice occasionally during cooking to keep it from forming lumps. I can't see any reason why rice should not be stirred during cooking. After 7 minutes, the rice will still be very slightly hard in the center. Test it by removing a sample with a spoon and biting into it. If you are satisfied, drain the cooking water through a sieve or colander and then place the sieve with the rice in it over the emptied pan. Pour boiling water from the teakettle through the rice to wash it; the water will collect in the pan. Then pour the collected water over the rice again. This will remove a lot of the excess starch, thereby giving you rice that's less fattening and rice that won't stick together like a great congealed mess. Serve on a warmed platter with a decorative wedge of lemon for each portion. It's not easy to keep rice warm; if I have to, I place the rice on a platter—I don't spread it out too much or it will dry out—and seal with aluminum foil over the whole platter, and then keep it warm in a low oven.

The final accompaniment is the popadams, if you are lucky enough to get hold of them. They are easy to prepare, just pour about ¼ inch *(3/4 centimeter)* of oil in a skillet and let it get hot enough so it just starts to smoke—approximately 375° F. *(190° C.)* if you have a proper thermometer—and then, using tongs, fry each one. It's a rush job—they take about 10 seconds a side and I usually prepare at least 2 per person, as they are popular. After the *briefest* of cooking, drain them on paper towels and serve immediately along with the rest of the meal.

For adventurous guests who are trying a curry for the first time, I always serve plenty of iced water, or a pitcher of chilled beer—though I'm told Indians never drink when eating curry.

Note: Popadams, Indian cakes made from lentil flour or cornmeal, can be obtained in specialty or ethnic food markets in major cities. When fried they become crisp, not unlike potato chips.

CHEESE POVERTY SOUFFLÉ

4 good helpings
Preparation time: 40 minutes

This recipe is an early Meg Horan, my mom. It's the most inexpensive meal she knows, and as we were growing up we were often fed this meal "to keep the wolf from the door." It became nicknamed "poverty pie" in our family and is, indeed, very nutritious and delicious. It's a good dish to serve to vegetarians with baked potatoes and a green vegetable.

Special equipment needed: a 2½-pint soufflé dish, a 2-quart heavy-bottomed saucepan, a wooden spoon, a cheese grater, a medium-sized stainless steel mixing bowl, a hand electric mixer or a medium-sized balloon whisk

Butter or margarine for greasing
4 tablespoons *(2 ounces; half a stick)* **butter**
3 level tablespoons *(¾ ounce)* **all-purpose flour**
½ cup *(4 fluid ounces)* **fresh milk**
1⅓ cups *(4 ounces)* **grated sharp Cheddar cheese**
3 *(2¼)* **tablespoons Parmesan cheese**
1 *(¾)* **teaspoon dry English mustard powder**
2 **large, fresh eggs at room temperature**
Salt and freshly milled pepper

METHOD: Preheat the oven to 375° F. *(190° C.)*, and then carefully grease the inside of a 2½-pint soufflé dish. (I think using a proper white soufflé dish is very important—you can get away with murder so long as the dish looks appetizing.)

Now melt the butter in a 2-quart, heavy-bottomed pan over a medium heat; don't let it burn. Add the flour and cook for two minutes, stirring. Add the milk all at once and keep stirring until all the lumps go. Turn the heat to low and add all but 1 *(¾)* tablespoon of the cheeses, and the mustard. Remove from the heat.

Separate the eggs, putting the whites into a clean, medium-sized stainless-steel mixing bowl and adding the yolks, one at a time, to the sauce and stirring them in, quickly, with a wooden spoon.

Now whisk the whites into a frenzy! The beaters of your hand mixer or balloon whisk must be absolutely clean. Remember, you're beating in the air until soft peaks form and you can tip the bowl upside down without the whites coming out. Don't overbeat, or you'll beat the air out.

Now pour one-third of the sauce mixture into the egg whites and gently combine. The word most recipe books use is "fold;" I can't think of a better word. I use a wooden spoon to do this. When loosely folded (by this I mean that you can still identify some of the egg white), add all this back into the sauce and again fold carefully. Swiftly pour the lot into the buttered soufflé dish, sprinkle the one *(¾)* tablespoon of reserved cheese over the surface, and bake for 30 to 35 minutes. Five minutes before the time is up, summon the troops. Soufflés cannot be kept waiting; they fall as soon as they start to cool, so the only way is to get everyone seated, knife and fork in hand, and then proudly produce your wonderfully risen soufflé and serve before it has a chance to fall.

JEAN'S LEMON MIDDLE

6 servings
Preparation time: 20 minutes
Cooking time: 1 hour and 15 minutes

The English often eat lemon desserts; their tartness is a good way to finish the meal. The base here is a pavlova, or meringue, which is easy to make *if* you measure the ingredients properly. The Lemon Middle filling is stolen from my friend Jean, who lives in Twickenham on the outskirts of London. It is a basic lemon curd (don't be put off by the name) — I use this as filling for cakes and as a hot or cold topping for ice cream. If you try any recipe in this book you should try this one — but follow the method exactly; no shortcuts, please.

Special equipment needed: a baking sheet, an electric hand mixer or large balloon whisk, a medium-sized metal bowl (stainless steel is okay), a metal tablespoon, a large saucepan, a wooden spoon, wax paper, fine grater, juice extractor

3 large, fresh egg whites at room temperature
1 cup *(7 ounces)* **superfine sugar**
¼ teaspoon cider vinegar
1 (¾) teaspoon cornstarch
LEMON CURD
2 large, fresh eggs at room temperature
1 large, fresh lemon (grate the rind, and squeeze the juice)
½ cup *(3½ ounces)* **superfine sugar**
4 tablespoons *(2 ounces; half a stick)* **butter**
½ pint *(8 fluid ounces)* **heavy cream, whipped (optional)**

METHOD: First lightly grease a baking sheet, then lay a piece of wax paper over it and grease the paper. Set the oven at 300° F. *(150° C.).*

In a very clean mixing bowl place the egg whites and whisk until soft peaks start to form (you've done enough whisking when you can tip the bowl upside down and the egg white holds firm). I use a hand electric mixer but you can use a large balloon whisk; if you use the whisk, don't forget that you are trying to beat air into the egg whites—that's what makes them go stiff. If you overwhisk you will then start to beat the air out again, so don't overdo it.

Now add the sugar (make sure there are no lumps) about ⅙ of a cup *(1 ounce or so)* at a go, whisking briefly after each addition. When you've added the last of the sugar, quickly whisk in the vinegar and cornstarch. The addition of these two ingredients will help to give your pavlova more stability and body.

Pour the whole lot onto the lined baking sheet and, with the aid of a metal tablespoon, spread into a circle of about 8-inch *(20-centimeter)* diameter. Try to use circular movements to spread the mixture, starting from the center and spreading outward.

Place in the oven, immediately turn heat down to 275° F. *(135° C.)* and bake for 1 hour. After the hour is up, turn off the heat but leave the pavlova there until the oven is completely cold—preferably overnight. Some people I know actually "cook" their meringues in their heated clothes-airing cupboards all day, but I think that's unhygienic, don't you?

When the meringue is completely cool, prepare the lemon curd. In a medium-sized metal bowl whisk the eggs and lemon juice together, and add the lemon rind and sugar. Add the butter in little pieces. Place the bowl so that it sits over a pan of simmering water. Stir occasionally until the curd thickens, about 10 to 15 minutes. Attend to the matter in hand and do not leave the stove or the mixture could break down and you'd have to start over. It will, like magic, become thick and creamy. Remove from the heat and cool.

When the curd is cool, carefully remove the wax paper from the pavlova and place it on a serving dish. Just before serving pour the cooled lemon curd over the meringue. To finish the dish and make it a hundred percent sinful, serve with whipped heavy cream. I find this lemon curd keeps well if refrigerated in a sealed container, and I quite often make it just so that I have something delicious to stick my fingers into when I feel like snacking.

CHELSEA BUNS

About 10 buns
Preparation time: approximately 3 hours, including rising time

The original Chelsea is an area of London that has rather a similar atmosphere to New York's Greenwich Village. Chelsea Buns are a must for anyone wanting to get to grips with food in London. You'll be able to buy them at many bakeries throughout England, but definitely in London. Bakeries are much the same as they are in major American cities. Some are just retail outlets for mass factory production and a few are the actual home of the bakery — the store in the front part, the bakery in the back. Survey the bakery scene carefully, as with pubs. You have only to enter the store to see whether there's evidence of baking on the premises. If you're not sure, ask. Buy only where they bake, fresh daily on the spot.

Any recipe involving yeast is a challenge to one's cooking ability but I see no reason why a complete novice can't do this recipe. The result is very rewarding and I would choose to make this recipe on a wet Saturday afternoon when nothing much was going on, as the main ingredients required are: time, patience, and close adherence to my instructions. The whole of your living space will be filled with a wonderful smell of fresh baking and you'll be amazed how people will appear from nowhere as you remove the finished products from the oven.

Finally, I have had a lot of trouble adapting this recipe to American ingredients, and I have decided this is because the flour available in the States is different; in England we would use a special "strong" baking flour, high in its gluten content, which is excellent for its baking quality. After much practice I have decided that Gold Medal all-purpose, enriched flour is the nearest equivalent.

Special equipment needed: a large china mixing bowl, a baking tin approximately 12 inches by 8 inches *(30 centimeters by 20 centimeters)* with 2-inch *(5 centimeter)* sides, 2 or 3 2-pint plastic or metal bowls, rolling pin (I use an old wine bottle if I can't find my rolling pin), pastry brush, a sharp 4-inch *(10-centimeter)* knife, a clean plastic garbage bag, a balloon whisk

3¹/₅ cups *(approximately 1 pound)* all-purpose flour (use Gold Medal)
1 *(³/₄)* level teaspoon salt
4 tablespoons *(2 ounces; ¹/₂ stick)* butter
¹/₂ cup *(3¹/₂ ounces)* superfine sugar
1 *(³/₄)* tablespoon dried yeast
¹/₃ cup *(2¹/₂ fluid ounces)* warm milk
¹/₃ cup *(2¹/₂ fluid ounces)* warm water
2 large, fresh eggs at room temperature, lightly beaten
Extra flour for rolling out

FILLING
1 cup *(approximately 6 ounces)* mixed dried fruit, chopped fine
¹/₃ cup *(approximately 2 ounces)* light brown sugar
¹/₂ teaspoon *(large pinch)* allspice
2 tablespoons *(1 ounce)* melted butter

TOPPING
²/₃ cup *(about 5 fluid ounces)* hot water
¹/₃ cup *(about 1¹/₃ ounces)* sifted confectioner's sugar

METHOD: Before you start, get everything ready. Measure the main ingredients. It will help if you make sure that all your equipment and ingredients are warm, particularly in winter. Think about a warm place between 65° F. and 75° F. *(19°C. and 24° C.)* where you can leave the dough to rise. In the past I have used my oven turned to the lowest possible temperature, but to be on the safe side, put dough in a turned-off oven with a pan of hot water on a lower shelf and keep replacing the water as it cools. Thoroughly wash your hands.

Sift the flour and salt into a large mixing bowl, preferably china (because it holds the heat), and rub in the butter with your fingers. This will take 5 minutes. Make a well in the center and put to one side.

Next, in a small mixing bowl dissolve the sugar and dried yeast in the combined milk and water, which you have warmed to hand hot. Hand hot is much hotter than you think—it should have a definite nip when you stick your finger in it. Set aside in a warm place for 10 minutes until small bubbles start to appear. (If they don't after 10 minutes, then your place isn't warm enough or your yeast is dead.) What you are doing is activating the dried yeast organisms by providing moisture, warmth, and food (sugar).

Pour the frothing yeast liquid into the well of the dry ingredients and add the lightly beaten eggs. Mix with a fork by first letting the sides of the well get mixed with the yeast/egg mixture, then slowly blending in the rest. It will be quite sloppy. Once you have it loosely mixed with a fork, use one hand for the mixing, holding the bowl with the other. Then turn the mixture out on a lightly floured surface. As the mixture is quite sticky, flour your hands lightly as well. Now knead.

Kneading is a process that involves working the dough: you take a handful of dough in each hand and push it away from you on the work surface so it gets flattened between the palm of your hand and the surface; then you gather the dough back into a ball; then turn a half-turn, and keep repeating. It takes practice but if you keep gently working it, adding a bit of flour to the work surface and your hands if the dough begins to stick, it will be okay.

Continue to knead for 5 minutes, then gather the dough into a ball and replace in the bowl (which has been washed and dried). Cover the bowl with a large, clean plastic garbage bag and leave it in your warm place to rise to double its size. This will take one hour; don't keep looking at it or you'll affect the temperature.

After an hour the dough will look waxy and spongy and will be much increased in size. Turn it out on a lightly floured surface and knock hell out of it with your knuckles to remove the air, and then roll it out (lightly flour your rolling pin) to an oblong shape approximately 12 inches by 6 inches *(30 centimeters by 15 centimeters)*.

Combine the dried fruit, sugar, and allspice in a small bowl. Brush the whole oblong surface of the dough with melted (but not hot) butter and then sprinkle the filling ingredients evenly over the whole area.

Starting on a long side, carefully roll up the dough neatly—like a jelly roll—and then, with a good sharp knife, cut cleanly into 1½- to 2-inch *(4- to 5-centimeter)* slices and place them in uniform rows on a greased baking tin. (You should get about 10 slices.) Arrange them about ¼ inch *(¾ centimeter)* apart so that as they have their final rising and bake they will join together. Cover again with the clean plastic bag and set back in your warm place until puffy. At this point preheat the oven to 425° F. *(220° C.)*. Bake the buns for 20 to 25 minutes till they are a golden brown color and smell irresistible.

Finally, as soon as you've removed them from the oven brush them with the combined topping ingredients to give them a shiny look. Remove from the tin and cool on a wire rack. Eat immediately with a nice cup of tea.

THE MIDLANDS

The Falkland Arms, Great Tew, Oxfordshire. A typical village scene in the Midlands — note the thatched roofs.

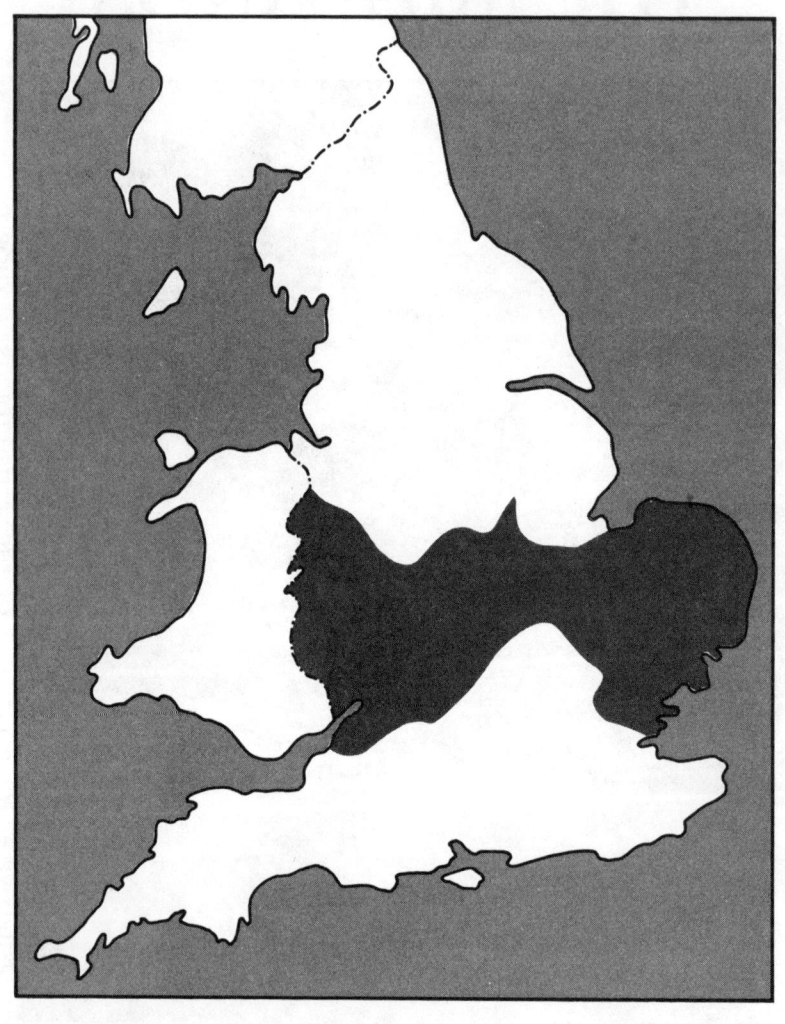

IF I WERE writing a sequel to "My Favorite Things" from *The Sound of Music*, these are some of my word associations with the area known as the Midlands: Oxfordshire, the Cotswolds, Gloucestershire, deep red stone, "spaghetti junction," Worcestershire sauce, thatched roofs, Shropshire, Tewkesbury Abbey, market day, the Royal Shakespeare Company at Stratford-upon-Avon, twisty roads.

The area is full of contrast and contains as much heavy industry as it does remote countryside. Birmingham, Coventry, and an area known as the Potteries are heavily industrialized. The Potteries is one of the most messed-up areas I know. Talk about industrial devastation! In order to give the world fine English china like Spode, Royal Doulton, and Royal Worcester, the area, rich in china clay, has been consistently and systematically excavated to the point where many of the buildings are tumbling down from lack of foundation support. To make matters worse the area is also rich in coal, though many of the mines are now closed—so there are hundreds of forgotten tunnels buried beneath the ground. It's hard to think that less than a hundred miles away you'll find the sleepy Cotswold area.

The British transport system serves this area well. Motorways, rail, and canals run right through the center. The drive from London to Manchester on the M1 and M6 will take you right slap through the middle of Birmingham—on stilts! If you had thought that English towns are all small and quaint, then driving through the center of Birmingham will give you quite a shock.

For an English town to be called a city it has to have a cathedral and a bishop. Many of the cathedrals and churches in this part of the world are old, famous, and have wonderful architecture. It is often possible to see many different building styles, indicating age, in one building. The ceiling fan vaulting you'll find in Tewkesbury Abbey is one of the best examples of "perpendicular" architecture you'll find anywhere in Europe.

Americans always want to visit Stratford and the Cotswolds (a range of hills in which you find many sleepy villages), and why not? Both are lovely places but there's more. Gloucester, Cheltenham, Banbury, Warwick, Oxford, Leamington Spa (a spa town is one that has a health spring rich in minerals), Buckingham, Leicester, Melton Mowbray—all market towns, meaning that on certain days of the week the market square is full of local farmers and small merchants selling their produce and merchandise from small covered stalls.

You can always tell when it's market day; there's a wonderful atmosphere of organized chaos and traffic congestion. Children running around, usually completely out of control, and hundreds of people milling about looking for a bargain. I always head for the food counters, as you might expect. Local produce is high on my list, but I'm as interested in the vendors as I am in their produce. Many of the vendors are there as a result of long-standing family tradition—market stalls are hard to come by and the right to a particular space in the market square is usually passed on from generation to generation. So if you get an opportunity to drop in on a market day, do so eagerly; many of these markets date back to medieval times and you'll be witnessing a sight that you might have seen, with few changes, hundreds of years ago.

If you buy anything, make sure you sample local dairy produce—especially the butter and cheese. You may even find a cheese and onion pie for sale, but until you get the chance, why not make one using my recipe on page 41?

RAREBIT CHEDDAR MELTS

1 serving
Preparation time: 15 minutes

Here I go again, fooling you into reading a recipe by changing the name of an old English classic, Welsh rarebit. I include it in this section as one area of the Midlands borders on Wales, from whence the dish originates; this snack is eaten all over England. There is some controversy whether the name is "rabbit" or "rarebit." I personally feel it's more likely to be "rarebit," as "rabbit" sounds too much like a mispronunciation. This is one of the best snack meals I know and can be made in a jiffy.

Special equipment needed: a small stainless steel mixing bowl, a large fork, a sharp 4-inch *(10 centimeter)* knife, aluminum foil

1 1/3 cups *(4 ounces)* grated sharp Cheddar cheese
1 fresh egg yolk at room temperature
2 squirts Worcestershire sauce
1/2 teaspoon *(large pinch)* dry English mustard powder
1 *(3/4)* tablespoon fresh milk
2 slices of your favorite bread
1 slice tomato for garnish

METHOD: Preheat your broiler.
In a small mixing bowl put the cheese, egg yolk, Worcestershire sauce, mustard, and milk and mix well with a fork. You'll find that the cheese does not readily accept the liquid; that doesn't matter—keep mixing and after a couple of minutes you'll get a sort of paste.
Now place the two slices of bread on a piece of aluminum foil and toast one side in the broiler. When the side is light brown, remove the slices and the foil from the broiler and put on a working surface. Turn the slices over so the untoasted sides face up and scoop the cheese mixture evenly over the surfaces of the two pieces of bread, making sure you cover all of each slice.

Return slices to the broiler for approximately 5 minutes until the tops are a lovely golden brown. (You use the foil to stop the melting cheese from dripping all over your oven.)

Garnish with a slice of tomato and eat immediately. Then prepare to make another batch—they're so good!

SAVORY CHICKEN PANCAKES

4 servings
Preparation time: for the pancakes, 30 minutes
for the savory chicken, 20 minutes

The English call crêpes pancakes. They are a lot of fun to make but require some practicing—and as with many kitchen procedures, practice makes perfect. The ingredients for making crêpes are not expensive so you can afford a few failures in order to perfect your technique. It is traditionally English to toss the pancake in the air as a method of turning it over so that the other side gets cooked. I can give you the guidelines, but even then there are days when I find my own crêpes stick for no apparent reason, even though I'm following all the rules, so don't get too upset if they don't turn out well the first time. The whole secret to successful pancake or crêpe making is in the skillet you use, the correct batter mixture, and the right amount of oil at the correct temperature. In the long run a heavy-bottomed 7-inch *(18-centimeter)* skillet that you *never* wash but always wipe out with kitchen roll (English for paper towels) and then lightly grease before storing in Saran wrap is the answer, but as a stopgap nonstick skillets do the job for a year or two before the bottoms buckle and the nonstick surface wears out. The savory pancake has started to appear on English menus only quite recently. You can make all sorts of fillings, but this is the one I like best. The leftovers from a roast chicken are ideal here.

Special equipment needed: a large mixing bowl, a balloon whisk or small electric hand mixer, a ladle, a heavy-bottomed 7-inch *(18-centimeter)* skillet, a 2-quart heavy-bottomed saucepan, wooden spoon, cheese grater, serving platter, aluminum foil, small pitcher for the oil, a Palate knife.

1 cup *(5 ounces)* all-purpose flour
2 large, fresh eggs at room temperature
1 cup *(8 fluid ounces)* water mixed with
⅓ cup *(about 2½ fluid ounces)* milk
2 tablespoons *(1 ounce)* lightly salted butter, melted
Approximately ½ cup *(4 fluid ounces)* light corn oil in a small heat-resistant pitcher

FILLING
4 tablespoons *(2 ounces, half a stick)* butter
3 level tablespoons *(¾ ounce)* all-purpose flour
2 cups *(16 fluid ounces)* fresh milk
⅔ cup *(2 ounces)* grated sharp Cheddar cheese (preferably Wisconsin)
2½ tablespoons *(1 ounce)* grated fresh button mushrooms
¼ cup *(2 ounces)* cooked white meat of chicken, roughly chopped
Salt (optional) and freshly milled pepper

METHOD: Into a large mixing bowl sift the flour, then make a well in the middle of the flour and break in the two eggs. With either a hand electric mixer or balloon whisk (or even a fork) start incorporating the eggs with the flour, taking the flour nearest the sides of the well first. As you progress you can start adding the milk and water. Ignore any lumps that form; they'll go away as you start to whisk. Make sure you include the mixture that gets stuck to the sides of the bowl. Whisk till the batter is smooth and creamy. You don't have to make this ahead of time and let stand—this is an old wives' tale that I've found makes no difference at all. When you're ready to make your pancakes, whisk in the melted butter.

Next, place your skillet on a high heat and pour in enough oil so that by tipping the pan the oil reaches all parts of the base and a half-inch *(1¼ centimeters)* round the sides. As the pan heats, the oil will thin; the pan will start to give off a bluish hazy smoke after about 3 to 5 minutes of heating. Pour back *all* the excess oil into the pitcher. (The purpose of the oil is to stop the pancake from sticking, and you don't need much.)

When the pan is really hot, pour in about 2 tablespoons *(1 ounce)* of batter. I do this with a ladle and guess at the amount. Now by quickly tipping the pan (holding it by its handle), distribute the batter to all parts of the base of the pan, and then immediately place it back on the heat to cook. It will only take about 45 seconds, and you can check it by carefully sliding a palate knife around the edges and looking underneath to see if it's golden brown. Now remove from the heat by firmly grasping the pan handle with one hand and carefully, firmly, and swiftly strike the pan handle lower down with the other hand, clenched, to dislodge the pancake. At this point, having loosened the thing, you can, if you wish, try flipping it. If you think you can do it, make sure there's an audience, as it looks very impressive if you catch it, but there's no need to flip it as it will be cooked through at this point. If you want to flip it, maneuver the crêpe, by holding the pan down and in front of you, so that it slides till its edge meets the lip of the skillet. Then in one fell swoop toss it three feet into the air and catch it (hoping to God that it's flipped itself in the process). Slide it off on to a plate, which you have warming over a pan of simmering water.

Repeat the process, always adding the oil and pouring it off. You should get at least 14 wafer-thin pancakes but at first you probably won't. These can be made the day before and stored, stacked and covered with aluminum foil, in the refrigerator. To reheat, warm them up in a low oven, still covered with the foil.

So you have your pancakes made—maybe you made them yesterday. Now for the filling. In a 2-quart heavy-bottomed saucepan melt the butter over a low to medium heat and add the flour all at once to make a "roux" (the French word for this mixture). Cook for 1 minute before adding the milk all at once.

Stir with a wooden spoon over a medium heat until the mixture starts to get thick, then beat more vigorously to remove the lumps. You need the consistency of heavy cream, so if your white sauce is a little thick add a little more milk to get the correct consistency. This is important—if the consistency is too runny the filling will run out of the pancake; too thick and it will be too dry to be palatable.

Add all the rest of the ingredients and cook on a low heat for a further 2 minutes, making sure you stir the mixture at the bottom and sides of the pan, until cheese is melted and everything heated through.

To assemble, put about two tablespoons of filling in the center of each pancake. Fold in half, then again in half, so you have the shape of a quarter of a circle. Some people prefer merely to roll them. Place on an ovenproof serving dish, cover with aluminum foil, and warm in the oven on a low heat for 10 minutes before serving—about three to each portion.

VEGETARIAN SHEPHERD'S PIE

4 servings
Preparation time: 45 to 60 minutes
Baking time: 20 minutes

When you ask someone, "What's English country cooking?" you expect them to reply, "Oh, well, things like shepherd's pie and bangers and mash and stuff like that." Well, you're beginning to discover that proper English cooking is a lot more than the old diehards. This recipe and method is taken from a recipe book of someone I greatly admire, but because I've adapted it for American measurements she's asked me not to use her name. She notes that it's just as good as, if not better than, the conventional recipe, which uses hamburger meat, and says that you don't have to be a vegetarian shepherd to enjoy this delicious meal.

Special equipment needed: a 2-quart heavy-bottomed saucepan, a heavy-bottomed skillet, a wooden spoon, a slotted metal spoon, a sharp 4-inch *(10-centimeter)* knife, a 12-inch by 8-inch *(30-centimeter by 20-centimeter)* glass ovenproof pie dish with 3-inch *(8-centimeter)* sides

1 cup *(7²/₃ ounces)* whole green lentils
²/₃ cup *(5 ounces)* green *or* yellow split peas
2²/₃ cups *(18²/₃ fluid ounces)* hot water
Butter or margarine
2 sticks celery, thoroughly washed and chopped
1 medium onion, peeled and chopped
2 carrots, peeled and chopped
½ green pepper, chopped
1 clove of garlic, peeled and crushed
½ teaspoon *(large pinch)* dried mixed herbs
¼ teaspoon *(pinch)* of ground mace
¼ teaspoon *(pinch)* cayenne pepper
Salt and pepper
½ pound *(225 grams)* tomatoes, peeled and sliced
TOPPING
1 small onion, peeled and diced
4 tablespoons *(2 ounces, half a stick)* butter
1½ pounds *(675 grams)* potatoes, cooked
2 tablespoons *(1 fluid ounce)* heavy cream
1 cup *(3 ounces)* grated sharp Cheddar cheese
Salt and freshly milled black pepper

METHOD: Wash the lentils and split peas, put them in a 2-quart saucepan with the hot water, and simmer gently, covered, for approximately 45 to 60 minutes, or until the peas and lentils have absorbed the water and are soft. Preheat the oven to 375°F. *(190° C.).*

While this is going on, melt some butter in a frying pan, add celery, onion, carrots, and chopped pepper, and cook gently until softened, then add these to the cooked lentil mixture after mashing it a little first. Add the garlic, seasonings, and salt and pepper to taste, then spoon the mixture into a large pie dish and arrange the sliced tomatoes on top (for help on how to peel tomatoes, see My Aunt Occie's Chutney, page 122).

Next prepare the topping. Soften the diced onion in butter in a small pan. Mash the potatoes, add the cooked onion, remaining butter, heavy cream, and grated cheese, and mix thoroughly with a wooden spoon. Season well, then spread on top of the ingredients in the pie dish. Bake for about 20 minutes or until the top is slightly browned. Tomato ketchup is a wonderful accompaniment.

CHEESE AND ONION PIE

4 to 6 servings
Preparation time: 40 minutes
Cooking time: 30 minutes

Of all the English recipes I know, this one for Cheese and Onion Pie seems to be my most popular in America. I associate this scrumptious savory pie with lazy picnics boating on the rivers at either Oxford or Cambridge, where you can rent what we call a punt. A punt is a long flat boat that is propelled by a long pole rather than oars.

A traditional English scene in the twenties could have been a college undergrad, gently and skillfully maneuvering his boat down river, while his lover hand-fed him tidbits like cheese and onion pie. The modern-day scene is much more riotous. If I have anything to do with it, I try to put a female in charge of the pole. The pole is very heavy, and you need a lot of experience before you can make the boat go in the direction you want. The result is one crash after the other, and with any luck at least one of these crashes results in a man or woman overboard. You can usually hear the laughter in the center of the town!

The only hard part of this recipe is making the pie crust, but if you follow my recipe and method you should produce a mouth-watering result.

Special equipment needed: 10-inch *(25-centimeter)* ovenproof glass plate (without sides), 1 large and 2 small mixing bowls, a cheese grater, a wooden spoon, a pastry brush, a sharp 4-inch *(10-centimeter)* knife, a rolling pin, a small saucepan, a potato masher, a sieve

PASTRY CRUST
2 cups *(10 ounces)* all-purpose flour
½ teaspoon *(large pinch)* salt
¼ pound extra-sharp Cheddar cheese, grated to make 1⅓ cups (see note)
½ cup *(4 ounces)* solid vegetable shortening at room temperature
3 *(2¼)* tablespoons (or more) ice water
Flour for rolling out
1 egg beaten with 2 *(1½)* tablespoons of milk to glaze crust
FILLING
2 medium baking potatoes, peeled
4 tablespoons *(2 ounces, half a stick)* butter
¾ pound extra-sharp Cheddar cheese, grated to make 4 cups (see note)
2 *(1½)* level teaspoons dry English mustard powder
2 *(1 fluid ounce)* tablespoons white wine
2 medium onions, peeled and thinly sliced

METHOD: The first thing to do is the pastry crust. Sift the flour and salt into a large mixing bowl and gently stir in the 4 ounces of grated cheese. Then in a smaller bowl place the shortening and 3 *(2½)* tablespoons of the flour mixture, and add the water. Beat this well with a wooden spoon, then transfer all of it into the larger bowl containing the remainder of the flour. With your fingertips rub the fat mixture with the flour for about three minutes. If you're skillful you'll be able to combine the mixture so it forms a ball, but if it doesn't you may add a little more water. Then cover with a plastic bag and place it in the refrigerator.

Now do the filling. Cube the potatoes and boil them in water in a small saucepan until soft but still firm; then drain thoroughly and allow the retained heat to evaporate the last of the water. Assemble the other filling ingredients.

Place the potatoes in a medium-sized bowl and mash them up with a masher until all the lumps have gone; add the butter, cheese, mustard, and wine, and mix well.

Lightly flour a working surface and your rolling pin. Divide the chilled pastry into two halves, return one half to the refrigerator, and roll out the other half carefully until it's a little larger than the base of your glass ovenproof plate. I know that to a novice this is easier said than done, but persevere! To transfer the rolled out pastry, merely roll the pastry around the rolling pin, then unroll it over the plate so that the plate is completely covered and the sides of the pastry hang over the plate slightly.

Preheat the oven to 350°F. *(180°C.)*.

Place a layer of sliced onions on the pastry base, leaving a ½-inch *(1½-centimeter)* border round the sides, then spread half the potato/cheese mixture over the onion. Repeat so you end up with (from bottom to top) onion, cheese, onion, cheese.

Now, with a pastry brush, moisten the border of the pastry base (which you have been careful to keep free of filling) with a little water. Roll out the other half of the pastry and transfer over the pie so that it will slightly overlap the base. Press the sides down firmly with your fingers and then cut the overlapping pastry with a sharp knife. I then make a pretty shell-like indentation round the edges with the thumb of one hand pressed against the thumb and forefinger of my other hand.

Lightly brush the surface of the pie with the egg/milk mixture and bake on the middle shelf of the oven for 30 minutes until the top is a light golden brown.

To give a final homemade touch I often reroll the pastry scraps and cut out 2-inch *(5-centimeter)* diamond shapes. I arrange them on the top crust of the pie before it goes in the oven, brushing a little of the milk/egg mixture on their bases to hold them in place.

Serve hot or at room temperature. This pie keeps, covered and refrigerated, for up to 3 days.

Note: I use Wisconsin Cheddar; it's the nearest to English Cheddar.

LEMON SURPRISE PUDDING

4 servings
Preparation time: 1 hour

This is a typical English pudding that's rather like a light cake with a lemon sauce. The surprise is that you pour the whole mixture into the baking dish, and when you take it out of the oven the cake and sauce have divided—the sauce is underneath. Anyone can make this; why not try it?

Special equipment needed: grater, 1 large and 2 small mixing bowls, a hand electric mixer/or a balloon whisk, a 1-quart soufflé dish, a juice extractor, a wooden spoon, a sharp 4-inch *(10-centimeter)* knife

4 tablespoon *(2 ounces, half a stick)* **butter at room temperature**
6 tablespoons *(approximately 3 ounces)* **superfine sugar**
2 **large, juicy lemons, zest and juice**
2 **large, fresh eggs at room temperature**
5 tablespoons *(approximately 1½ ounces)* **self-rising flour, sifted**
⅔ cup *(approximately 5 fluid ounces)* **fresh milk**

METHOD: With a wooden spoon beat the butter, sugar, and lemon zest in a medium-sized china bowl until it's soft and well mixed together. Separate the egg yolks from the whites and then beat the yolks, one at a time, into the sugar/butter mixture. Fold in the flour and then slowly add the milk and lemon juice alternately.

Preheat the oven to 350°F. *(180°C.)* Butter a 1-quart soufflé dish. In a separate, clean bowl whisk the egg whites till soft peaks form and fold them into your main mixture. It might look a bit curdled; don't worry, that's how it's supposed to look.

Pour the whole lot into the prepared soufflé dish and bake on the middle shelf of your oven for 40 to 45 minutes until the top is golden brown. Serve immediately. There! A lovely, heart-warming, hot winter dessert—very English.

SYLLABUB

6 servings
Preparation time: 30 minutes
Waiting time: 8 hours
Chilling time: 2 hours

Syllabub is a very old English frothy drink. I like to serve it as a dessert, just for a change. It was all the rage in England with the Elizabethans around the mid-1600s. I'd like to be able to tell you this recipe has been handed down within my family from generation to generation, but it hasn't. The original version was made from warm milk freshly milked from the cow and then mixed with ale, cider, or wine. In the 1700s the word became loosely associated with any creamy alcoholic whip. I suppose it might be the equivalent of an alcoholic milkshake.

In America we'll never quite be able to duplicate a proper syllabub because proper double cream isn't readily available here, so we have to use the best quality heavy cream (preferably not ultrapasteurized) we can find.

Special equipment needed: 1 large and 1 small stainless steel bowl, a hand electric mixer or a balloon whisk; a sharp 4-inch *(10-centimeter)* knife, a chopping board, 6 1-cup, stemmed wine glasses

²/₃ cup *(approximately 5 fluid ounces)* sweet, white wine
1 *(³/₄)* tablespoon Bristol cream sherry
2 *(1¹/₂)* tablespoons brandy
1 fresh, juicy lemon or orange
2 *(1¹/₂)* tablespoons superfine sugar
¹/₂ pint *(8 fluid ounces)* heavy cream

METHOD: In a large stainless steel bowl place the wine, sherry, and brandy. Then carefully peel the zest part of the rind *only* from the lemon or orange, add half the zest and all the juice to the liquid, and put the other half of the zest aside, wrapped in foil. Leave overnight! Yes, overnight. The oils (the taste) from the zest have to mingle with the liquid. The following day remove the zest and discard.

Stir the sugar into the liquid until it dissolves.

In a separate, clean bowl whip the cream (use cream straight from the refrigerator) until stiff and then fold into the liquid. Spoon the whole lot into the wine glasses. Leave to stand in the refrigerator for 2 hours, and top each glass with super-thin shreds of the lemon or orange peel that you put to one side.

THE HOME COUNTIES

"Over!" After the bowler has bowled six balls, the fielding team cross the cricket pitch to the opposite position. This is a typical Sunday scene in the Home Counties and was taken at Abinger Hammer on their village green.

PHOTO BY CHRISTOPHER HORAN

ABOUT the only time you'll ever hear this part of England being referred to as the Home Counties is when you listen to BBC news programs. At the close of the news they'll say "And now for the weather. All areas will have rain, and the Home Counties will get more than the rest of the country this evening. . . ."

The Home Counties are the counties that surround London. In the United States, the areas of Connecticut, New Jersey, and New York bordering New York City and known as the Tristate Area would be the equivalent.

The Home Counties include Kent, Surrey, Berkshire, Middlesex, Hertfordshire, and Essex. (When you arrive at Heathrow you land in Middlesex; when you arrive at Gatwick you land in Surrey.) These areas are, in effect, where the greater part of the London work force go home each night after work and were originally known as the "home circuit," named after the assize circuit that a traveling judge would follow to preside over cases in the outer London area. I once heard a woman declare at a rather classy dinner party, "Well, dears, I live in the champagne belt of London." This area probably contains many of England's wealthiest families.

There is great rivalry between people who live north of the Thames and those who live south. Quite honestly both areas have their good and bad points. If I list them, I perpetuate the myth, so you'll have to discover them for yourself.

As I was born and raised in Hertfordshire, this is the region I know the best, so let me focus in on Herts (pronounced "Harts"), as it's locally known.

When I was a kid in the 1950s the area was virtually rural. Our little hamlet is known as Croxley Green, and a very pretty place it is too. It is, however, located on a main road called A404 and is very close to Watford, the nearest large town. Like all towns Watford, the heart of the printing industry, has exploded into action. Tons of people, motorways, stores, shopping malls—you name it, Watford's got it. It's just like any rural American city. This growth affected my sleepy village. The A404 started to get too busy for comfort—huge tractor-trailers would plough through relentlessly both day and night. The sleepy village green (it was "common land"), which once was used to graze a local farmer's sheep, became invaded by weekend tourists getting a look at real trees and natural grass. For this area, like many other of the Home Counties bordering on London, is about the first bit of proper English countryside you hit when leaving London (eighteen miles distant) as you drive north.

If you stay in London, you'd be well advised to take a train, rent a car, hire a cab—but get there, and have lunch at a country inn situated in the Home Counties. Naturally I'd prefer you to visit Hertfordshire, but a thirty-mile trip in any direction out of London will lead you to an exciting adventure. The best inn I know to visit in Hertfordshire is called the Royal Standard of England, near Beaconsfield (on the A40 or M40) in a village called Knotty Green, a thirty-mile journey from London. It's one of the oldest pubs in England and the lunchtime pub food is excellent.

CREAM OF WATERCRESS SOUP

4 to 6 servings
Preparation time: 45 minutes

In the area where I was raised, Rickmansworth in Hertfordshire, watercress is grown in beds of fresh water supplied by the river Chess. A little further upstream the same river supplies water to a trout farm. As a child I often used to wonder what would happen if the trout escaped, swam downstream, and ate the watercress. I have always found watercress eaten on its own to be a rather uninteresting vegetable, but when made into a soup it shines.

Special equipment needed: a 4-quart heavy-bottomed saucepan with a lid, a sharp 4-inch *(10-centimeter)* knife, a blender, a ladle

4 tablespoons *(2 ounces)* **lightly salted butter**
2 bunches nice, green *fresh* **watercress**
2 medium potatoes, peeled and roughly chopped
3 large leeks *(approximately 450 grams 1 pound,)*, **thoroughly washed, roughly chopped**
3½ cups *(28 fluid ounces)* **chicken stock or water with 3 chicken bouillon cubes**
Salt and freshly ground black pepper
⅔ cup *(approximately 5 fluid ounces)* **heavy cream**

METHOD: Melt the butter in a 4-quart heavy-bottomed saucepan. Remove the stems of the watercress (saving one sprig per person for final garnish) and add the tops, along with the other vegetables, to the butter. Stir, cover with a lid, and sweat over low heat for about 15 minutes.

Add the stock and bring to a simmering point for a further 10 or 15 minutes until the veggies are soft.

Put the whole lot through a blender, blend lightly, then return to the pan and adjust the seasoning to taste.

Serve hot or chilled. Before serving, put a slurp of heavy cream in each serving dish, pour on a portion of soup, then garnish with a sprig of watercress.

JERUSALEM ARTICHOKE SOUP

6 servings
Preparation time: 45 minutes

This is *the* soup to end all soups, as far as I am concerned. It's got a lovely unique flavor, is very simple to make, and is as good hot as it is chilled. If you've never made soup before, start with this recipe. The only difficult thing about the preparation may be obtaining Jerusalem artichokes (often called "sunchokes"), but they can be found in produce stores, health food stores, and many supermarkets.

A Jerusalem artichoke is a *completely* different vegetable from a conventional artichoke, part of the thistle family, of which one eats the heart with melted butter or other sauce. No, a Jerusalem artichoke is not an artichoke at all; it is the tuberous root of a sunflower plant and resembles a small knotty potato or, even more markedly, fresh ginger root.

Special equipment needed: a heavy-bottomed 4-quart saucepan, a blender, a sieve, bristle scrubbing brush, ladle

1 pound *(450 grams)* Jerusalem artichokes
2 tablespoons *(1 ounce)* lightly salted butter
5 cups *(40 fluid ounces)* milk
Salt and freshly ground black pepper
½ pint *(8 fluid ounces)* heavy cream
6 *(4½)* teaspoons chopped chives

METHOD: To start with, scrub the artichokes with a stiff bristle brush, getting as much dirt out of those odd little knots as you can. It is not necessary to peel them—"Thank God," I hear you say, for peeling these weird-shaped objects would be a nightmare.

In a large, heavy-bottomed saucepan melt the butter over medium heat and add the artichokes and milk. Bring to the boil, being careful to be around when the boiling point is reached. Otherwise it will rise up over the sides of the pan and make an awful mess. As soon as it boils, reduce the heat to a simmer and cook until the chokes have lost their shape—that usually takes about 25 minutes. (Treat as if you were trying to overboil a potato.)

Put the whole lot through a blender and strain back into the pan through a sieve. Now add the salt and pepper to your taste. You may need to adjust the consistency by adding more milk, but it should be quite thick.

When serving, put two tablespoons of the cream in the base of a soup dish and pour on a portion of soup with a ladle. (The soup can be served either hot or chilled.) Garnish with a teaspoon of chives sprinkled over the surface, sit back, and receive compliments. Tell the guests that it's very hard indeed to make.

HONEYDEW MELON WITH GINGER

6 servings
Preparation time: 10 minutes
Chilling time: at least 1 hour

This isn't really cooking at all—I include it more as a serving idea, because melon is very often served this way in England. The sweet honeydew melon is really nice only if it's properly ripe (a greenish-yellow on the inside), chilled, and served with freshly ground ginger. The way to tell if it's ready is by pressing with your two thumbs at the pointed end of the melon. If it gives ¼ inch *(¾ centimeter)* it's ready to eat.

Special equipment needed: a sharp 8-inch *(20-centimeter)* knife, a wooden cutting board, 6 8-inch *(20 cm)* flat glass or china serving plates, 1 small attractive serving bowl, a dessert spoon

1 large honeydew melon
2 fresh juicy oranges
4 *(3)* tablespoons freshly ground ginger
4 *(3)* tablespoons superfine sugar

METHOD: Cutting a melon is more difficult that you might think. Take your knife and carefully make a cut into the center so that the blade touches the two pointed ends—that is, lengthwise, never crosswise. Then make a similar cut from the opposite side, and the melon will be in two halves. You do this so that the blade won't carry the pips (pits) through the second half.

Now, with a dessert spoon, remove all the pits and fibers from each half. Divide each half into three equal sections, again lengthwise. Make your slices from the outside skin to the center.

Prepare each section for serving. You do this by making a cut right in the center, lengthwise from point to point, being careful that the point of your knife doesn't pierce the outer skin. Next make a cut as close to the skin as you can so that you nearly remove the skin from the flesh, leaving the flesh attached for the last half-inch. Now make 6 equal crosswise cuts, and if you've followed correctly you'll have 14 bite-sized portions and the section will still have its original shape.

Finally, carefully slide each cross-section a half-inch in alternating directions from each other so that side edge looks like the battlement of a castle. Take a slice of orange and make a cut from the center to the outside and then twist it over the melon, for decoration.

Chill for at least one hour. Serve as an accompaniment a mixture of the sugar and ginger. The sugar is really there for its grittiness quality more than its sweetness—your melon will be quite sweet enough.

CHRISTOPHER'S VEAL

2 servings
Preparation time: 30 minutes

You're in a hurry, and somehow you have to produce a wonderful gourmet meal. You've not done a lot of cooking but you want the food to be good. Your date is turning up in ten minutes for a romantic dinner, which is still not prepared. What do you do? My veal is the answer. If you prefer you can use chicken breasts or pork chops (pork requires longer cooking than chicken or veal). Veal is not as readily available in England as it is in the States; it is considered rather a luxury, and also there are many English who have strong moral objections to eating veal.

Special equipment needed: a heavy-bottomed skillet, a wooden spoon, a sharp 4-inch *(10-centimeter)* knife

2 tablespoons *(1 ounce)* butter/or margarine
2 cloves garlic, peeled and very finely chopped
2 scallops of veal, approximately 6 ounces each
1 cup *(8 fluid ounces)* red wine
½ cup *(4 fluid ounces)* heavy cream
Salt and freshly ground black pepper

METHOD: In a heavy-bottomed skillet melt the butter or margarine and then toss in the garlic. Sauté the garlic for 1 minute, stirring with a wooden spoon. It will start to brown slightly, but do not allow it to burn; that would affect the flavor. On a wooden chopping board flatten the veal with a mallet or large chef's knife and add to the skillet so both pieces lie flat. Cook each side for 5 minutes.

Pour on the wine and continue to cook for 5 minutes more. The wine should be bubbling; if it isn't, turn up the heat till it does. Then remove the pieces of veal and put to one side (veal doesn't require a lengthy cooking).

Continue the reducing of the wine until it has almost evaporated. Then stir in the heavy cream and return the veal to the pan for its final heating. Add salt and freshly ground black pepper to taste and quickly serve. The result will be very professional.

I serve this dish with rice and a green salad. If you are using chicken breasts or pork chops use a white wine, not too sweet. And if you use pork chops, you must increase the cooking time substantially. Depending on their thickness, it will take at least 30 to 45 minutes to cook pork chops thoroughly. You want them tender, with no pink showing when you cut into one.

The Home Counties

DUCKLING WIZARD

2 servings
Preparation and cooking time: 3 hours

You often see the word Aylesbury associated with duckling on English menus, and that's because ducks are bred right there in the town of Aylesbury, Buckinghamshire. Just as in the States, it's easier to obtain a frozen duck than a fresh one in England. I have no problem in using frozen duck, excepting that it does take a long time to defrost — at least 24 hours at room temperature.

Duckling can be delicious but only if really crisp. To achieve this crispness you'll need to allow 40 minutes per pound in a medium oven — that's twice as long as you'd allow for chicken. Ducks contain a tremendous amount of fat, and if you're cooking a duck for the first time you'll be amazed how much fat drips off the bird.

In England, duck is often served with a tart orange sauce; the acid in the sauce goes well with the rich, dark meat. Other classic duck accompaniments are watercress, "game chips" (very thin, homemade potato chips), or proper roast potatoes, a thin gravy, and sometimes a light stuffing (dressing) like sage and onion.

Finally, a duckling never gets very large, and has more bone than flesh, so although half a duckling per person seems like a huge portion when you present it on a plate, it's not a lot by the time you've picked your way through it. As you will see, there's loads of time for you to get all the little meal details done, because cooking a duck dinner takes quite a long time but not much effort — you're not exactly tearing around the kitchen. So plan to make this meal when you've plenty of time and are perhaps going to do other household jobs.

Special equipment needed: a large roasting pan with 2-inch *(5-centimeter)* sides, a trivet, a large sharp chef's or french knife, a sharp 4-inch *(10-centimeter)* knife, a heavy-bottomed 1-quart saucepan with a lid, a large wooden chopping board, aluminum foil, a wooden spoon, a suction baster

1 4-pound *(1800-gram)* duckling (approximate weight)
Salt
1 fresh juicy orange, quartered
SAUCE
2 tablespoons *(1 ounce)* butter
2 *(1½)* tablespoons dark brown sugar
4 *(3)* tablespoons very good quality orange marmalade preserve
Zest (finely diced) and juice of 1 large juicy orange
Zest (finely diced) and juice of half a juicy lemon
½ to ¾ cup *(4 to 6 fluid ounces)* water or good strong chicken stock (stock is better)
GARNISH
2 large orange slices
2 small bunches watercress

METHOD: Before you do anything, be sure that if you are using a frozen duck it has had at least 24 hours at room temperature to defrost—no emergency methods like microwaves or hot water, please!

If you are not experienced at producing a roast meal, consult the recipe on page 198 (Roast of Chicken), as the order of tackling things is the same though the timing is different.

Preheat the oven to 375°F. *(190°C.)*. Remove from the duck's cavity the plastic bag containing the giblets. Rub the inside with salt and then tuck the orange quarters inside the bird. (I do not recommend that you stuff the bird; stuffing slows the cooking process and often means you get a burnt outside and an undercooked inside. Stuffing is best made separately.) Loosely cover the duck with aluminum foil and place it on a trivet in a roasting pan with 2- or 3-inch *(5- or 8-centimeter)* sides. The trivet prevents the bird from sitting in a lot of grease.

Place in the oven, and set your timer for one hour. During this first cooking time you can prepare other accompaniments—the vegetables, an appetizer, a dessert—and set the table. One of the jobs you can do now is the sauce.

You do this by simply melting the butter in a 1-quart heavy-bottomed pan over a low heat. Then add the brown sugar and cook for 30 seconds. Now add the marmalade preserve (a good one is dark in color and has plenty of thick peal in it), plus zest and juice of the orange and lemon. Stir with a wooden spoon and then add approximately a third of the stock or water and bring to the boil. At this stage the sauce will be too thin; eventually it needs be the consistency of a thinnish syrup. You control the consistency by evaporating (by boiling) to make it thicker or by adding more liquid to thin it. At this point in the preparation of the meal I usually put the sauce to one side, cover with a lid, and correct the consistency just before I'm ready to serve the duck.

After the first hour, remove the foil from the bird, and reduce the oven temperature to 325°F. *(165°C.)*. Quite a lot of fat will have been rendered so pour it off and discard it. Return the duck to the oven for the remainder of the cooking time—1 hour and 40 minutes if the bird weighs approximately 4 pounds *(1800 grams)*. No basting is required at all, but every 20 minutes or so you'll need to remove the fat collecting in the bottom of the roasting pan. I do this with the help of a suction baster.

The bird is ready when it smells irresistible and when the outside skin is a very deep golden brown—if you're worried that it's burned, it's probably perfectly cooked. Remember duck is very unappealing if it's not absolutely crispy on the outside.

Place the bird on a firm chopping surface. Using a very large, sharp french or chef's knife, position the blade over the center of the breast so that it also sits between the legs (i.e., lengthwise), and holding the knife firmly with one hand, *smash* the top of the knife with a clenched fist so that you drive the knife right through the center of the bird, splitting it in half. If you have weak hands, do the smashing with a mallet or get someone else to oblige.

Now you need to remove as many of the bones as you can. The rib cage, some of the wing bones, and the breast bone will come away quite easily—the difficulty is that it's all too hot, so be warned. I use my hands—they've been burned so often they're more or less as tough as asbestos. Anyway, do the best you can with the help of a tea towel or paper towels.

Prewarm an oval serving platter. Place each portion, skin or "presentation" side up, on the platter. Place a slice of orange on each portion, then pour the sauce over and serve. You can, if you prefer, serve the sauce separately. A small bunch of washed watercress for each portion also helps to add color to this lovely meal.

WHISKEY CREAM PIE

4 to 6 servings
Preparation time: 20 minutes
Chilling time: at least 1 hour

My original recipe calls for "digestive biscuits" and golden syrup. Neither is readily available in the United States so I've adapted to the nearest thing and think the result is possibly better. In place of the Scotch you could use almost any liqueur except those that are very sweet.

Special equipment needed: 10-inch *(25-centimeter)* glass flan dish with 1-inch *(2½-centimeter)* medium-sized heavy-bottomed saucepan, a rolling pin, a baking sheet, a hand electric mixer or a medium-sized balloon whisk, 1 large and 1 small stainless steel mixing bowl

PIE SHELL
4 tablespoons *(2 ounces, half a stick)* **butter**
1 *(³/₄)* **tablespoon maple syrup**
½ pound *(225 grams)* **graham crackers**

FILLING
½ pint *(8 fluid ounces)* heavy cream
1 large egg at room temperature
⅓ cup *(about 2½ fluid ounces)* runny honey
2 *(1½)* tablespoons Scotch whiskey
GARNISH
3 *(2¼)* tablespoons peeled, sliced almonds

METHOD: This dessert is so easy. First, make the shell. (I do not approve of using premade graham cracker bases—not as delicious and no scrunchiness.) In a medium-sized heavy-bottomed saucepan melt the butter over a low heat, add the maple syrup, and put to one side for a moment. On a working surface distribute the graham crackers and smash them by rolling a rolling pin over them like a steam roller (it's tidier if you do this on a large piece of wax paper). Gather the crumbs, add them to the butter/syrup mixture, and mix very well with a wooden spoon. You will be thinking there's not enough moisture to bind them, but don't worry, there is.

Next, press this mixture into a 10-inch *(25-centimeter)* glass flan dish with a metal tablespoon, making sure you press well into the corners and the crust is evenly dispersed. Stick it in the freezer compartment for a few minutes while you get on with the filling.

In a large mixing bowl whisk the cream till stiff. Thoroughly wash and dry the beaters. Separate the white of the egg from the yolk and place the white in a smallish bowl. You don't need the yolk. Whisk the white till soft peaks form and you can tip the bowl upside down without the white falling out.

Now stir the whiskey and honey into the cream with a metal spoon. Fold in the egg white and pour the whole lot over the chilled flan base.

Finally spread the almonds on a baking sheet and place under the broiler for a few minutes—keep turning them to brown them. Be careful, they burn easily. When they are cool (don't they smell good?) sprinkle them over the pie and refrigerate for at least an hour. The whole operation takes me 20 minutes, what about you?

SHERRY TRIFLE

6 servings
Preparation time: 2 to 3 hours, including chilling

When I first made what I know to be a proper trifle in America, my class looked at me as if I were crazy, that is, until they tasted the result. Rather like making, say, a green salad, there are no hard and fast rules for the ingredients. This is the version I prefer. The most difficult thing to master is the making of the custard, because we are using egg yolk to thicken. This means the heat has to be applied rather gently or the whole thing turns into scrambled eggs and has to be thrown away or fed to the dog. So follow carefully, no failures please.

Special equipment needed: a medium-sized stainless steel bowl, a hand electric mixer or a balloon whisk, a 1-quart heavy-bottomed saucepan, a 4-quart heavy-bottomed saucepan or a double boiler, wooden spoon, sieve, 6 stem wine glasses with a 1-cup capacity or a 2-quart glass bowl, a pastry bag and large star-shaped tube or a dessert spoon, a grater

3 large, fresh eggs at room temperature, separated
3 *(2 1/4)* tablespoons superfine sugar, sifted
2 cups *(16 fluid ounces)* fresh milk
2 tablespoons *(1 ounce)* unsalted butter
Ingredients for the gelatine
2 12-ounce packets frozen strawberries or raspberries, defrosted
1 11-ounce can whole segments of mandarin oranges
Approximately 7 ounces pound cake (stale is okay)
1/2 cup *(4 fluid ounces)* sweet sherry
1/2 pint *(8 fluid ounces)* heavy cream
GARNISH
10 candied cherries
1 ounce refrigerated bittersweet chocolate

METHOD: To start, make the custard. Place the egg yolks and sugar in a medium-sized stainless steel bowl and whisk until the color becomes lighter—2 minutes if you use an electric hand mixer. In a heavy-bottomed small saucepan heat the milk to just short of boiling, *but do not let it boil.* While the milk is heating, bring 2 inches *(5 centimeters)* of water to boil in a large pan in the base of your double boiler. Then add the hot milk to the egg mixture (N.B., not the other way round) and gently combine with the whisk. Place the bowl so it sits over the pan of gently simmering water, but don't let the water touch the bottom of bowl. Do not leave the range; instead, patiently keep stirring the custard until it thickens slightly. Most recipes are very unspecific as to how long this takes. I've waited around hours for something dramatic to happen and it doesn't. You'll just notice that the mixture coats the back of a spoon better after about 10 minutes of gentle heating than it did before. When you're satisfied that it has in fact thickened, stir in the butter and carefully cover the surface with a piece of wax paper and put to one side to cool.

Now make the gelatine. In England we call it "jelly." Of course one can buy packets of chemically flavored gelatine, but I want you to control the flavor yourself. It's dead easy. First, make sure your frozen fruits have defrosted properly (you'll notice that quite a bit of juice has collected). Place them in a close-meshed sieve and *gently* work the fruit through the sieve, using a wooden spoon, so that the juice runs into a small bowl underneath. Do not overwork the pulp or the pips (pits) will get into the juice, and we don't want our guests picking the pits out of their teeth, do we? It's the juice we want, 2 cups of it in fact. You won't have quite enough liquid from the berries so make it up with the juice from the mandarin oranges. Now place the 2 cups of liquid in a small saucepan, sprinkle the gelatine over it, and heat gently, stirring with a wooden spoon, until all the gelatine has dissolved. This won't take more than 2 or 3 minutes; there's no need to bring the fruit juice anywhere near the boil. Put to one side to cool.

Start to assemble the trifle. Break up the cake into approximately 1-inch (2½-centimeter) cubes with your hands and place cubes in the bottom of 6 1-cup capacity stem wine glasses. Distribute over the cake 1/2 cup *(4 fluid ounces)* of sherry. Divide the mandarin oranges among the glasses and pour 1/6 of the gelatine mixture over each. Refrigerate until the gelatine has set — perhaps a couple of hours. If you prefer you can make one large trifle rather than individual ones. In this case use a 2-quart glass bowl. I prefer to make individual servings — they look prettier.

When the gelatine is completely set, pour the custard over it. The custard will by now be much cooler and therefore thicker, though it will never actually set like the gelatine. In a clean medium-sized bowl whip the heavy cream until stiff and then carefully spoon the cream over the surface. (I prefer to use my pastry bag with a large star-shaped tube.) Finally, decorate with cherries and grate the chocolate over the top. Keep refrigerated till required. This dessert will keep for two days and can be made in advance as far as the cream. Whip that, put it on, and do the garnishing just before you serve. Do not freeze the finished trifle — fresh egg products don't freeze very well.

THE NORTH OF ENGLAND

A typical scene of the bleak moorland areas you'll find in the North of England.

PUBLISHED WITH KIND PERMISSION OF THE BRITISH TOURIST AUTHORITY.

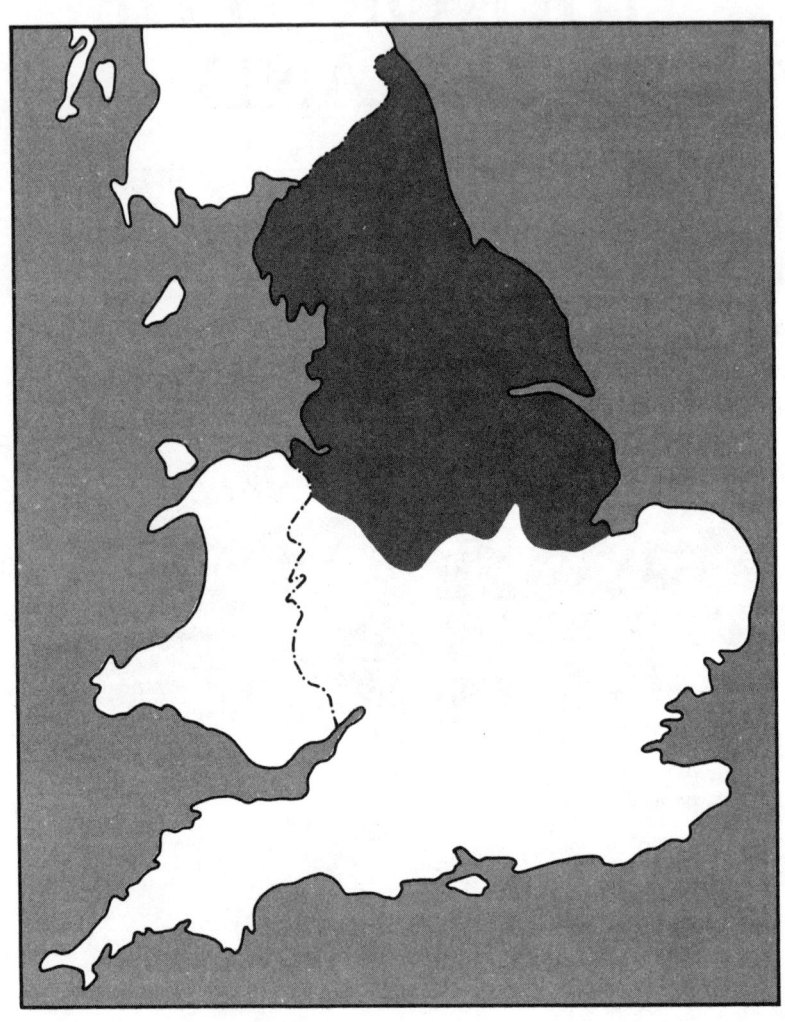

THE counties included in this section are Cheshire, Derbyshire, Nottinghamshire, Lincolnshire, Merseyside, Greater Manchester, Humberside, Lancashire, Cumbria, Dumfries and Galloway, Durham, Northumberland, and North, South, West, and East Ridings of Yorkshire.

This area is historically the industrial hub of England and the origin of mass production as we know it today. When you drive through this part of England you will observe a great change in the countryside. The Cheshire plains are a minute version of the American Midwest. The farms grow wheat, barley, corn, and a variety of animal fodder and fruits and vegetables. Cheshire dairy herds are famous for their rich creamy products, and the cheese produced here is famous throughout the world.

As you travel north, the plains will give way to more hilly countryside. You will find the typical northern town like Sheffield or Blackburn nestled in a valley surrounded by hills. As you stand perched on the tops of these undulating ranges of hills (which include the Pennine range) you will see many little industrial towns, each specializing in its own product.

The area exploded into industrial activity in the early nineteenth century largely as a result of cotton. The constant damp atmosphere combined with strides made in water- and steampower and the availability of cheap labor meant that Britain could produce competitive cotton products for the world market. The area is also rich in coal.

Each township would specialize in the production of coal, cotton spinning, garment manufacturing, cutlery, iron and steel production, and so on—not unlike the industrial centers of America. The towns would be interdependent on each other for the raw material needed to make their products.

In total contrast, the countryside areas are remote and very beautiful. You will find much of the area similar to scenes described in the Brontë novels: beautiful yet bleak moors with very little vegetation. You will also find the people robust and warm-hearted. Many of the families have grown up here under extreme hardship with very poor living conditions—people have been very much exploited for the sake of industrial growth. It is largely as a result of these people's toil that Great Britain became a world power, for they provided Britain with its stable, productive industries.

Included in this region is a very special area, extremely popular with Americans, called the Lake District, a group of small and large lakes surrounded by minimountains. The largest, Lake Windermere, is the center of activity and became a fashionable resort for the rich mill owners and industrialists of the last century. If your travels take you to this part of England, you would do well to try out one of England's famous "B & B" places.

"B & B" means bed and breakfast, and you will find many of these signs outside small homesteads as you drive along. They are inexpensive and you will often be included as part of the family. Many B & B's offer an evening meal as well. Your room will be simple and clean; you probably won't have your own bathroom, but you will sample real home cooking of the area, and have a wonderful chance to really get to know the local people. The B & B business has sprung up from a need to increase income—the man perhaps having been unable to find enough work to support his family. His wife, ever resourceful, puts her skills and house to work, usually only during the summer months. You may well find that you're actually sleeping in the master suite of the house, the family having been banished to less luxurious accommodation in the kitchen or a camper in the garden.

Due to the very damp, chilling weather and the economics of the area, you will find the food hot and filling! Meat and potato pies (more potato than meat), fish and chips, thick soups are the order of the day. Food designed to fill a lot of mouths inexpensively, food that is energy- and heat-producing, food high in carbohydrate content.

When these dishes are well made they are excellent and well worth having up your sleeve for those cold winter nights when your budget is a little low (or you are living very quietly, as my mother puts it when she's spent the housekeeping money on something she shouldn't have). When they are badly made they are quite frightful. I think you will enjoy good results if you follow these simple instructions.

LEEK AND POTATO SOUP

6 large servings
Preparation time: 45 minutes

In some circles a similar version to this simple yet delicious soup is known as vichyssoise—its main ingredients are leeks and potatoes, staples for northerners. It's very easy to make and is as good in the winter as it is in the summer. In hot weather it can be served chilled, though I must admit I've never been able to get used to cold soup.

Special equipment needed: blender, a 4-quart heavy-bottomed saucepan with lid, a ladle, a small hand balloon whisk

2 tablespoons *(1 ounce)* lightly salted butter
1 *(³/₄)* tablespoon pure corn oil
1 medium onion, roughly diced
1 clove garlic
4 cups *(32 fluid ounces)* homemade chicken stock
2 pounds *(900 grams)* good quality potatoes, peeled and diced into 1-inch *(2¹/₂-centimeter)* cubes
3 large leeks or 6 small (the larger are about 1 inch *[2¹/₂ centimeter]* thick), thoroughly washed and roughly chopped
2 whole bay leaves
Salt and fresh ground black pepper to taste
Water to adjust consistency at the end
1 cup *(8 fluid ounces)* heavy cream, lightly whipped (optional)
2 *(1¹/₂)* tablespoons finely chopped chives (optional)

METHOD: In a 4-quart heavy-bottomed saucepan, melt the butter and oil, and add the onion. While it is cooking over low heat, place your clove of garlic on a flat surface and on it lay flat your largest chef's knife. In one swift blow hit the knife with a clenched fist, holding the handle of the knife with the other hand; this will crush the garlic and make it easy for you to remove the outer shell from the flesh. Chop the flesh into the smallest pieces you can and add to the onions.

After 5 minutes the onions will be translucent. Add stock, potatoes, leeks, and bay leaves. Turn up the heat and bring to the boil, then reduce heat to a rolling simmer for 15 minutes, or until the potatoes are soft (a knife should cut them with ease).

Remove from heat and allow to cool before putting the whole lot through a blender (remove the bay leaves first). Be careful! Operate your blender responsibly. If you fill the blender's container more than half full you could wind up washing your English soup off the wall.

Once blended, return soup to the saucepan and add salt and pepper to *your* taste (remember some people don't like too much salt). Correct the thickness by adding water so that you get the consistency of slightly whipped heavy cream. At this stage you can freeze the soup for up to three months.

Serve either hot or chilled. When you're ready to serve, place in each soup dish two tablespoons of heavy cream and pour on a portion of soup (a ladle will make this easier). Sprinkle on the surface of each portion about a teaspoon of the chives.

You can change the taste of this soup by adding other background vegetables such as celery, carrots, turnips, and swede (English for rutabaga), but you will probably need to pass the soup through a sieve after you have blended. If next time you want a greener soup, add more leeks. If you want a different consistency, adjust the quantity of potato.

HAM AND ASPARAGUS ROLLS
with Deviled Cheese Sauce

4 appetizer servings, 2 rolls each portion
Preparation time: 25 minutes

This is a lovely dish to learn. It is easy to prepare and trebles as a snack or a main course. The word "deviled," in English cooking, usually means the addition of English mustard, which makes the dish hot. (I've come to the conclusion that Americans use the word "spicy" as we English would use the word "hot.")

Special equipment needed: cheese grater, 1-quart heavy-bottomed saucepan with a lid, wooden spoon, a baking sheet approximately 10 inches by 15 inches *(25 centimeters by 38½ centimeters)* with ½-inch *(1¼-centimeter)* sides, flat oval serving dish

4 tablespoons *(2 ounces, half a stick)* butter
3 level tablespoons all-purpose flour
2 cups *(16 fluid ounces)* fresh milk
1⅓ cups *(4 ounces)* sharp Cheddar cheese (preferably Wisconsin) grated
3 level teaspoons English mustard (Coleman's is the best)
Salt and freshly ground pepper to taste
1 15-ounce can good-quality whole, green asparagus spears or 16 to 24 spears fresh asparagus of uniform size, blanched in boiling water until tender
8 thin slices cooked ham, sliced from a rectangular block (so that you get slices about 5 inches by 4 inches *[13 centimeters by 10 centimeters]*)

METHOD: In a heavy-bottomed 1-quart saucepan melt butter over medium heat. Stir in the flour all at once with a wooden spoon (in French cooking this is called making a roux) and cook for 30 seconds, stirring all the time. Now add all the milk and stir slowly. At first this will look like a mess, but keep stirring and as the milk heats up it will begin to combine with the butter and flour mixture to make a sauce. The hotter the milk gets, the more it will blend. When the mixture starts to bubble, beat hard for 30 seconds with the same wooden spoon to remove the lumps (sometimes impatience drives me to use a balloon whisk). At this point the sauce should be smooth and coat the back of a spoon evenly and thickly. Turn down the heat to low and stir in the cheese and mustard with a wooden spoon. Once the sauce is made it burns easily, so make sure you stir *all* the sauce at the bottom of the pan. A proper heavy-bottomed pan will help to prevent burning. Now add salt and pepper to your taste, remove from heat, and cover with a lid.

Preheat your broiler. Drain the asparagus and *carefully* remove the spears from can; don't break them. Lay out each piece of ham on a clean working surface and divide the asparagus among the ham pieces. You should have 2 or 3 spears for each piece of ham. Then roll up as if you were rolling up a man in a carpet. Arrange the rolls on a baking sheet and then spoon on the sauce so that each one is well covered.

Put under the broiler until the sauce starts to brown and bubble. Serve immediately on an oval flat serving dish.

If you want to prepare this ahead of time, do everything up to pouring the sauce over the rolls. Do that bit a few minutes ahead of serving. The sauce will keep for 24 hours (completely cover the surface with wax paper and refrigerate when cool).

SCOTCH EGGS

4 servings
Preparation time: 45 minutes

History doesn't tell us whether in fact this delightful way of doing eggs actually originated in Scotland, but as the North of England borders on Scotland it seems appropriate to slide them in here. You will find Scotch eggs served in most pubs throughout Britain, and they are a lovely item for a picnic. The hardest thing about this dish is making sure that the egg doesn't pop out through the sausage meat during deep-frying. If you follow these directions exactly you'll have no problems.

Special equipment needed: a deep-fryer or a 4-quart heavy-bottomed saucepan, a high temperature thermometer, slotted spoon, paper towels, rolling pin

4 medium eggs at room temperature
1 pound *(450 grams)* **bulk pork sausage**
1 cup *(5 ounces)* **all-purpose flour seasoned with a little salt and freshly ground pepper**
2 eggs, lightly beaten
1 cup *(8 fluid ounces)* **milk**
2 cups *(about 8 ounces)* **fine, dry breadcrumbs (If you've time make your own from stale bread, dried in the oven, and whizzed through a blender)**
Oil for deep-frying (I use 100% corn oil because it reaches a higher temperature before burning)

METHOD: First boil the 4 eggs. "Easy," I hear you say. But it's surprising how many people can't do this. Pierce each egg with a pin at its rounded end. Place them carefully into a pan and cover with cold water. Bring to the boil and when the water is really bubbling, immediately cover with the pan lid and remove from the heat. Leave them for 10 minutes. Then run cold water over and around the eggs in the pan for 2 minutes. While the water is running onto them crack them so that some of the moisture get in. You will now find the eggs easy to shell. You will also find your egg is perfectly cooked, the white firm and the yolk firm but not too dry, and there will be no nasty green mark between the yolk and white.

Divide the sausage meat into four equal pieces and roll each out on a lightly floured surface into 5- or 6-inch *(13- or 15-centimeter)* circles.

Now get the production factory going. (Be prepared for a bit of mess.) Prepare three bowls: the seasoned flour in one, egg/milk mixture in the second, and breadcrumbs in the third. Dip a shelled egg into the egg mixture, then in flour. Repeat with each shelled egg. Now place each egg onto a circle of sausage meat and bring up the sides to enclose egg completely. Hold it in both hands and squeeze gently to eliminate the air. Dip each ball into the egg mixture and finally roll each in the breadcrumbs.

Heat the oil to 375 to 400°F. *(190 to 200°C.)*. Fry 2 eggs at a time until each egg is a deep brown all over, about 10 minutes. (If you've not enough oil to submerge them, make sure you turn them to ensure even cooking.) Don't let the oil get too hot. Be careful! Deep-frying can be dangerous—oil plus sausage balls should not reach more than halfway up the sides of the pan. If the oil is too deep, it can sometimes boil over when you introduce the egg, and then ignite or just make a terrible mess over the stove.

Remove with slotted spoon and drain on paper towels. Repeat with remaining 2 balls. To serve as a main course dish, half each ball; as an appetizer or cocktail munchie quarter each ball. An appropriate accompaniment would be English mustard. Can be made three days ahead and refrigerated but not frozen.

MEAT AND POTATO PIE

6 large servings
Preparation time: 40 minutes
Cooking time: 90 minutes (30 minutes if using a pressure cooker)

Just because this is called a pie, don't be put off. I don't know anyone who doesn't like "meat and tatty pie," as this dish is affectionately called in the Manchester area. Like most British pies, it can be made ahead of time and finished off at the last moment. The dish traditionally uses a cheaper cut of beef (hence the long cooking time) because meat is very much more expensive in England, but you could use a better-quality steak and cook the meat for less time.

Special equipment needed: a heat-resistant 3-quart rectangular glass casserole measuring 12 inches by 8 inches *(30 centimeters by 20 centimeters)*, 2 egg cups, rolling pin, large mixing bowl, a 4-quart heavy-bottomed saucepan, a pastry brush, rolling pin

3 *(2¹/₄)* tablespoons corn oil
2 pounds *(900 grams)* lean shin beef (leg of beef) chopped into (1-inch) cubes
2 medium onions chopped
2 bay leaves
1 clove garlic, peeled and finely minced
1¹/₂ to 2 pints *(24 to 32 fluid ounces)* water
2 *(1¹/₂)* teaspoons Worcestershire sauce
¹/₃ cup *(about 2¹/₂ fluid ounces)* red wine
2 pounds *(900 grams)* good quality, firm potatoes, peeled and cubed
Salt and freshly ground black pepper
4 *(3)* teaspoons cornstarch mixed with a little water in a cup to make a paste

SHORT CRUST PASTRY

2½ cups *(12½ ounces)* all-purpose flour
1 cup *(8 ounces)* solid vegetable shortening
1 *(¾)* teaspoon salt (optional)
¼ cup *(2 fluid ounces)* ice water

METHOD: In a large heavy-bottomed saucepan, heat the corn oil over high heat for 3 or 4 minutes. Carefully add the meat and cook (still on a high heat) so that the meat quickly browns and seals all over. This usually takes about 6 to 10 minutes; you'll need to stir with a wooden spoon so that all parts of the meat get exposed to the heat. Don't worry if at first particles of the meat stick to the bottom; they'll loosen after a few minutes' cooking. Now stir in the onions, bay leaves, and garlic and cover with a lid. Continue to cook for a further 5 minutes.

Now add the water, Worcestershire sauce, and wine—there should be enough liquid so that the meat is covered plus an inch. Bring to the boil and then reduce heat to a rolling simmer. Cover and cook for at least 75 minutes, checking from time to time to be sure there is enough liquid, and stirring occasionally so that the bottom doesn't burn. The meat is ready for the next stage when it is tender and the cooking process has broken down the collagen content of the meat—the part that makes it tough. You may well find that you have to cook for longer; it all depends on your meat and how long it was hung before you bought it. This whole process is reduced to a 15-minute operation if you use a pressure cooker.

While the meat is cooking, prepare the pastry and potatoes. As the pastry likes to relax before being rolled out, do it next. Measure out the flour and put to one side. In a large mixing bowl place the fat, salt if you're using it, water, and 3 *(2¼)* heaped tablespoons of the flour you have put to one side. Beat vigorously with a wooden spoon till all is well blended (or as they say in the north, "Knock hell out of it!"). Now you have to be gentle. Add the remainder of the flour all at once and mix together with your fingertips until it all sticks together. If you are having problems, then you may add up to 2 *(1½)* more tablespoons of water, but no more. Remember that if you overwork the pastry at this stage it will shrink and be tough when cooked. Combine into a ball, cover with a slightly dampened tea towel, and put in the refrigerator.

Next, peel and cube the potatoes, cover them with water in a pan, add salt, bring to the boil, and cook until you can just poke a knife into them—about 10 to 15 minutes after the water boils. As soon as they are cooked, take the whole pan to the sink and run cold water through them for about 5 minutes, then drain. This will cool them and immediately stop the cooking.

When you are satisfied that the meat is cooked, strain off and reserve the liquid. Place the meat in the casserole dish, add the potatoes, and return the liquid to the pan. Over low heat add the cornstarch paste a little at a time; you probably won't need all of it. Keep adding (stirring all the while) until the liquid thickens to the consistency of heavy cream. Check the taste; if you feel salt and pepper are required, add them now. Pour the gravy over the meat so that the meat and potatoes are covered; you may not actually need all this sauce.

In the middle of the casserole dish place 2 egg cups, upside down and 4 inches *(10 centimeters)* from each other. On a lightly floured surface roll out the pastry to about 1 inch *(2½ centimeters)* larger than the dish. Brush the rim of the casserole with a little water to help the pastry stick to the sides. Transfer the pastry to cover the pie (the easiest way to do this is to carefully roll the pastry around the rolling pin, then unroll it over the length of the dish); the egg cups will help to prop the pastry up. Press the sides down snugly around the rim, and pierce the pastry with 2 little slits to let the steam escape.

At this stage you can keep your pie for up to 24 hours in the refrigerator (cover the pastry with dampened wax paper to keep it moist). You could also freeze it, but you would have to have used a dish (say a foil container) suitable for the freezer. If frozen, allow at least 12 hours of defrosting at room temperature.

At serving time, preheat your oven to 325°F. *(165°C.)* and cook until the pastry is light brown. Remember that everything inside the pie is cooked, so you only have to heat it through. To complete the course serve with a green vegetable or salad and you'll have a perfectly balanced meal.

FISH AND CHIPS

4 large servings
Preparation time: 40 minutes

I just have to include this because it is often on menus in America and rarely is it cooked right. How it gets so messed up by professionals is a mystery to me, as it's a dish anyone can make with minimum effort. The English traditionally eat fish and chips from newspaper. The "chippy" (a fish and chip vendor) wraps them in it, and, for me, the newsprint provides an extra flavor that's probably quite unhygienic, but special. You may be interested to know that for many northerners, fish, chips, and peas is a staple meal and almost by accident happens to be, nutritionally, a perfectly balanced combination. The "chippy" is now being undermined by fast food hamburger joints springing up everywhere.

Special equipment needed: a 4-quart heavy-bottomed frying pan (for frying the fish), a deep-fryer or a large heavy-bottomed saucepan (for frying the potatoes), a good sharp 4-inch *(10-centimeter)* knife, a balloon whisk or a hand electric mixer, a large mixing bowl, a cooking thermometer

1½ pounds *(675 grams)* decent firm potatoes, washed and peeled
2 pounds fillets of cod or scrod
Seasoned flour for dredging
Oil for deep-frying

BATTER
1 medium-sized fresh egg at room temperature
1 cup *(8 fluid ounces)* water
1 cup *(5 ounces)* self-rising flour
½ teaspoon *(large pinch)* salt (optional)
Freshly ground pepper

METHOD: When you've finished preparation of this meal it has to be eaten immediately, so start cooking exactly 40 minutes before you're ready to eat. First slice the potatoes into long sticks about ¼-inch *(¾ centimeter)* thick; the length will depend on the size of your potato. You will find a sharp knife a great asset in this operation. If you first take a thin slice off the potato you will find it sits flat on a working surface, making slicing the remainder of the potato less hazardous to the safety of your fingers. Try and make the sticks the same size so they will cook evenly. Put them in a bowl and cover with cold water to soak (this will help to remove some of the starch and give you a crispier and less fattening french fry).

Now prepare the batter. Simply break the egg into a large mixing bowl and lightly whisk with the water. Still whisking, add the flour, a little at a time. A blender will ease the operation, but if you've only a balloon whisk, be sure to beat out the lumps of flour so that you finish up with a smooth consistency. Add salt and freshly ground pepper and put to one side.

Thoroughly wash the fish fillets under cold running water. As you are washing, check to be sure that all the bones have been removed. (*Always* wash fresh fish before preparing.) You now want to divide the fish into 8 equal pieces—2 per serving. Sometimes the pieces you have bought may not conveniently divide into 8; you will have to use your judgment. Carefully dry with paper towels and dredge each piece in the seasoned flour, shaking off the excess.

Heat oil in your deep-fryer (if using a 4-quart saucepan, 1 pint oil will be enough) to 375 to 400°F. *(190 to 205°C.).* At the same time heat up in a heavy-bottomed frying pan about 1 inch *(2½ centimeters)* of corn oil to the same temperature. While the fat is slowly getting up to temperature, drain the potatoes. Be careful to get as much of the moisture of them as possible—use paper towels. As they dry, deal with the fish. When the oil in the frying pan is at the right temperature take each piece of fish and dip it in the batter mixture you put to one side. Allow the excess to drip back into the bowl and gently immerse the fillet in the hot oil. You shouldn't try to cook more than two or three pieces of fish at a time or you will reduce the temperature too much and the result will be soggy. The inside of the fish will be cooked when the outside batter is a mid to light brown. Fish, being almost pure protein, cooks quickly.

Turn on your oven to low so that you can keep the cooked pieces of fish warm while the other bits are cooking.

The french fries are easy to do. Take two handfuls of your chipped potatoes and carefully release them into the deep-fryer. Again, if you overload the deep-fryer you will reduce the temperature and the result will be soggy, so do the potatoes in two or three batches. When golden brown, remove with a slotted spoon so that you can shake off the excess oil, and turn onto paper towels.

The English like to eat fish and chips with tartar sauce, and also delight in throwing tomato ketchup all over. It is also traditional to eat the dish with "mushy" peas. These are dried peas that have soaked and then cooked so much that they almost turn into a sort of pea soup; they're very good.

One final word of advice. This last-minute type meal takes experience—the timing is very difficult to get right. I often call the family for dinner and then find the fries aren't done. Experiment, but not on guests.

TUNA NOODLE DOODLE

2 humongous servings
Preparation time: 30 minutes

This recipe is not English, nor is it a "gourmet" meal. Cooking from scratch is all very nice and something I'm committed to, but we all have our weak moments when a can has to come to our aid. I stole it from you Americans (how do you like that), but it's one I've come to like, and feel sure that if the northerners were introduced to it, it would be a firm favorite. I learned it from my friend Ross, who sometimes lives on it for a week, hot or cold. It's very easy to make and costs next to nothing. If this is the first time you've picked up a recipe book, I suggest you start with this easy and delicious dish. The wonderful thing about the meal is that you only have one pan to wash.

Special equipment needed: a large heavy-bottomed saucepan, cheese grater, a wooden spoon

1 quart water *(32 fluid ounces)*
2 cups *(4 ounces)* noodles (egg noodles are best)
2 tablespoons *(1 ounce)* butter or margarine
1 medium onion, finely diced
1 6½-ounce *(195-gram)* tuna in water
1 10¾-ounce *(305-gram)* can condensed cream soup (chicken or mushroom are my favorites)
1⅓ cups *(about 11 fluid ounces)* milk (just fill the soup can)
⅔ cup *(2 ounces)* grated sharp Cheddar cheese (optional, to make the "deluxe" version)

METHOD: Bring the water to the boil and toss in the noodles. Simmer until they are soft to the center, about 10 minutes. Scoop one out, blow on it, then eat it to see if it's cooked.

Drain and put noodles to one side. In same pan (don't wash it) melt the butter and add onion. Cook on low heat for 5 minutes, stirring occasionally. Now dump in: noodles, drained tuna, soup, and milk, and heat, still stirring occasionally to make sure the heat gets through.

Serve when hot, and for the "deluxe" version sprinkle the grated cheese over each portion. What could be easier? And if you eat a salad on the side you again have a nutritious, well-balanced meal.

BAKEWELL TART

6 servings
Preparation time: 15 minutes
Cooking time: 30 minutes

This dish was, as a legend has it, invented by mistake. A cook at the Rutland Arms, Bakewell (in the heart of the North Country) misunderstood her mistress's instructions and instead of adding the butter, eggs, and sugar to the pastry to make a jam tart (another English dessert), she rolled out the pastry, smeared jam on it, and spread the egg mixture on top. The guests that evening (possibly including Jane Austen) raved about it, and a dessert was born. In case you're thinking that Bakewell might be horrid because of its name, it's one of the loveliest little northern towns you'll ever visit.

Special equipment needed: a 9-inch *(23-centimeter)* diameter round cake tin with 1-inch *(2½-centimeter)* sides, a rolling pin, a balloon whisk or a small hand, electric, mixer, large mixing bowl, wooden spoon

PASTRY

2½ cups *(12½ ounces)* all-purpose flour
1 cup *(8 ounces)* solid vegetable shortening (I use Crisco)
1 *(large pinch)* teaspoon salt (optional)
¼ cup *(2 fluid ounces)* ice water

FILLING

3 medium-sized eggs at room temperature
½ cup *(3½ ounces)* superfine sugar
½ cup *(4 ounces)* butter at room temperature
¾ cup *(approximately 3 ounces)* ground almonds
2 *(1½)* heaped tablespoons good-quality strawberry preserves

METHOD: Make the pastry first. Measure out the flour and put to one side. In a large mixing bowl place the fat, water, and 3 *(2¼)* heaped tablespoons of the flour you have put to one side. Beat vigorously with a wooden spoon until all is well blended. Then carefully add in the rest of the flour, rubbing the mixture between your fingertips until it all sticks together. You can add up to 2 *(1½)* more tablespoons of water to help, but no more. Remember that if you overwork the pastry at this stage it will become tough, and shrink when cooked. Combine into a ball, cover with a damp tea towel and place in the refrigerator.

Preheat the oven to 400°F. *(205°C.)*. Beat the eggs and sugar together until creamy (this takes 3 minutes). Add the butter in small pieces, and the almonds, and continue to beat for another minute until all is combined. Set aside.

On a lightly floured working surface, roll out the pastry into a circle so that it's 3 inches larger than the baking tin, and about ⅛ inch *(½ centimeter)* thick. Lightly grease the tin, making sure you smear a very thin film all over the inside. Now transfer the pastry to the tin by carefully rolling it around the rolling pin. Be careful, it's not always easy; but if the pastry breaks a bit, don't worry—you can do a repair job when it's in the tin. Now with your hands fashion it to the inside of the tin, making sure it reaches inside the corners. Cut off the excess pastry with a knife. You will have pastry left over; roll it into a ball and freeze for next time.

In a small saucepan gently melt the jam so it will spread more easily. Distribute the jam evenly over the pastry in the tin and then cover the preserve with the egg mixture. Now bake in the center of your oven for 25 to 30 minutes— it's done when the filling has set and is a mid to deep brown all over. If it starts to brown on one side and not the other, turn the pie halfway through cooking (if you have to do this, do it quickly or all the heat will escape). This means that you'll have to keep an eye on it while it's in the oven.

I usually serve this with whipped heavy cream—mmmmmm, delicious! Not unlike pumpkin pie but with a lovely almondy flavor.

SHORTBREAD WITH CUMBERLAND RUM BUTTER

Makes about 15
Preparation time: about 10 minutes
Baking time: 30 minutes

These cookies are an old English favorite—I associate them with Scotland. They are even better than those expensively packaged cookies you buy in supermarkets, and are an ideal accompaniment for afternoon tea or as a cookie to eat with ice cream. I like to eat them with Cumberland rum butter. Try it, you won't be disappointed.

Special equipment needed: a cookie sheet, wooden spoon, a 3-inch *(8-centimeter)* crinkled cookie cutter, a wire tray for cooling, flour sifter, hand electric mixer (optional), rolling pin, china or glass bowl, wax paper, small heavy-bottomed saucepan

½ cup *(4 ounces, 1 stick)* unsalted butter at room temperature
⅓ cup *(about 2 ounces)* superfine sugar
1¼ cups *(6 ounces)* all-purpose flour, sifted
Superfine sugar for dusting
CUMBERLAND RUM BUTTER
1 cup *(8 ounces, 2 sticks)* unsalted butter
2¼ cups *(1 pound, 450 grams)* old-fashioned dark brown sugar
¼ teaspoon *(pinch)* grated nutmeg
⅓ cup *(about 2½ fluid ounces)* dark Jamaican rum

METHOD: First preheat the oven to 300°F. *(150°C.)*. Now make the shortbread. In a large bowl beat the butter (to be used as a dip or spread) with a wooden spoon till it's soft and continue beating while you add the sugar and then the flour. It will get hard to handle. Don't worry, just bring it together with the spoon and get it into a ball with your hands. Now transfer to a working surface that has been lightly dusted with superfine sugar. Then quickly and lightly roll out about ⅛ inch *(½ centimeter)* thick (you may need to dust the rolling pin with sugar too).

With the 3-inch *(8-centimeter)* cutter cut out the cookies and place on the cookie sheet. Bake on a high shelf in the oven for approximately 30 minutes, until they are a *pale* golden color, no darker. Cool the cookies on a wire rack and dust them with some superfine sugar. Then, when cool, store in an airtight container so they won't go soggy.

Now for the Cumberland rum butter. Melt the butter in a small heavy-bottomed saucepan *on a low heat*. As this is happening, put the sugar in a large mixing bowl and remove all lumps by pressing them out with your hands or a wooden spoon. Add the nutmeg. Pour on the rum and mix well. Pour on the melted butter and stir in well. Now turn into a glass or china bowl, cover the surface with wax paper, and when cool place in the refrigerator till required. There now, easy.

YORKSHIRE DESSERT

4 servings
Preparation time: 5 minutes
Cooking time: 15 minutes

I've changed the name to fool you into reading this recipe, in the hopes that you'll try it. It's really Yorkshire pudding—but served as a dessert. You can, if you wish, use this recipe for proper Yorkshire pudding to be served with rare roast beef. They used to make this because it's rather filling and would be served *before* the meat, so guests wouldn't eat so much meat, as it's expensive, especially in Yorkshire. I want you try it as a hot dessert—and I'm going to Americanize it by suggesting that you serve it with warmed Vermont maple syrup. You need to be organized for this dish if you are going to serve it to guests. Make the batter before you sit down to eat the main course, and then cook it while you're scurrying around the kitchen making the coffee and throwing the dishes into the sink or dishwasher. The "popovers" *must* be eaten as soon as they come out of the oven, while they are crisp.

Special equipment needed: a large mixing bowl, a balloon whisk or a hand electric mixer, a 12-hole popover tin, a ladle

1 cup *(5 ounces)* all-purpose flour, sifted
1 large egg at room temperature
½ cup *(4 fluid ounces)* milk
⅓ cup *(approximately 2½ fluid ounces)* water
2 *(1½)* tablespoons light vegetable shortening

METHOD: First make sure your oven is hot, say 425°F. *(220°C.)*. Then in a large bowl place the flour. Make a well in the middle in the flour, break the egg into it, and beat. Slowly add all the milk and water and beat to a smooth consistency. Some people maintain that you have to make the batter well ahead of time and then let it stand, but I've not found this necessary.

Now place a little of the shortening in each of the holes of the popover tin — about half a teaspoon in each — and put the tin in the oven for 2 minutes so the shortening melts.

Now remove the tin from the oven and place it on a low flame on top of the stove. Distribute the batter in each popover hole. I use a ladle to do this — less mess. As you pour in the batter it will sizzle. Be careful; it's quite easy to burn yourself during an operation like this (remove children and animals from the kitchen).

Put popover tin in the hot oven and bake about 15 to 20 minutes. The "popovers" will rise dramatically and be crisp and brown on the top. Serve immediately with some warmed maple syrup. Lovely!

RICE PUDDING

6 servings
Preparation time: 25 minutes

As English as apple pie! Something strike you as wrong? Of course. You'd say as American as apple pie. Well, in England we think we invented it. Seriously though, I don't want to start the breakup of diplomatic relations. My point is that apple pie is as popular in England as it is in America. So is rice pudding. This ad (see opposite page) appeared in the 1920s version of *Mrs. Beeton* and manages to capture, somehow, the aura surrounding childhood meals when my parent's generation was young and people like Christopher Robin were eating meals with Alice.

In my camp there is only one way to make a creamy rice pudding these days, and that's using a pressure cooker. If you

RICE PUDDING

Rice Pudding! We have all been *made* to eat it —"yes, if you sit there all afternoon." Thousands of children, we have been told so often, would be glad of it.

Have you ever had rice pudding made with Nestlé's Milk? Looks like a pudding made with cream! Tastes like a pudding made with cream! Doesn't look like a swimming bath with the rice swimming around. Very rich! Very nutritious! And the "skin"—the colour of autumn. Make a rice pudding with Nestlé's Milk next time. It will be a pudding and not a punishment.

LET'S PRETEND!

ALL CHILDREN NEED milk, but some don't like it. But milk can be turned into a real treat by spreading NESTLÉ'S MILK on bread and calling it "WHITE JAM." NO CHILD CAN RESIST IT.

PUBLISHED WITH KIND PERMISSION OF WARD LOCK LIMITED, LONDON.

A lovely ad which appears in the 1920s edition of Mrs. Beeton's Cookery and Household Management. *I find the insight the text gives into British middle-class life in the 1920s fascinating.*

don't have one, then don't attempt to make it—the conventional oven or stove-top methods are slow and produce a horrible, often burnt, version. Many people seem to have a horror of using a pressure cooker, but if you think you are responsible enough to use a gas range, then you have what it takes to use a pressure cooker. Take the time to read the manufacturer's instructions until you become familiar with your invaluable kitchen gadget.

Be sure you use round-grain rice. This has a completely different quality from the long-grain rice you serve with savory meals. The round grain is rounder and whiter.

Special equipment needed: a pressure cooker, a wooden spoon, a small sharp knife

2 tablespoons *(1 ounce)* unsalted butter
4 cups *(32 fluid ounces)* fresh milk
2/3 cup *(about 5 ounces)* round-grain rice
1/4 cup *(1 3/4 ounces)* sugar
A small piece of lemon rind
1/4 teaspoon *(small pinch)* fresh ground nutmeg
1 13-ounce can evaporated milk

METHOD: Remove the trivet from your pressure cooker and then melt the butter. Add all the milk and bring to the boil. Add the rice, sugar, lemon rind, and nutmeg. Return to the boil and *just* as the milk starts to rise reduce the heat so that the milk settles down to a rolling boil at the bottom of the pan.

Then, *without altering the heat*, place the lid on the pressure cooker and set to the highest pressure (15 pounds per square inch). When steam starts to escape, indicating that the correct pressure has been reached, and you hear that familiar noise you associate with pressure cooking, time and cook for 12 minutes.

After 12 minutes take the pressure cooker carefully to the sink and run cold water over the outside of the canister until the pressure is completely gone. (Lifting the weight very, very slightly will tell you whether there is still pressure there; if steam still escapes, then continue to run cold water over till it's all gone.) You can then remove the weight completely and safely open the lid. Stir the pudding well with a wooden spoon and then return to the heat, uncovered, and simmer until a *thick* creamy consistency is reached by evaporating more of the liquid, if necessary.

Finally add the can of evaporated milk, stir, and serve. Rice pudding will keep well in a sealed container in the refrigerator for up to 3 days. Do not freeze.

This is my sister Sarah's range. It's called an AGA—they are very common in English country kitchens and can be fired by gas, coal, or oil. They are wonderful to cook on.

THE SOUTH OF ENGLAND

A sleepy village scene in the South of England. Notice the real Tudor-style buildings: the chimneys and beam work in the walls are indications of this.

PHOTOGRAPH BY CHRISTOPHER HORAN

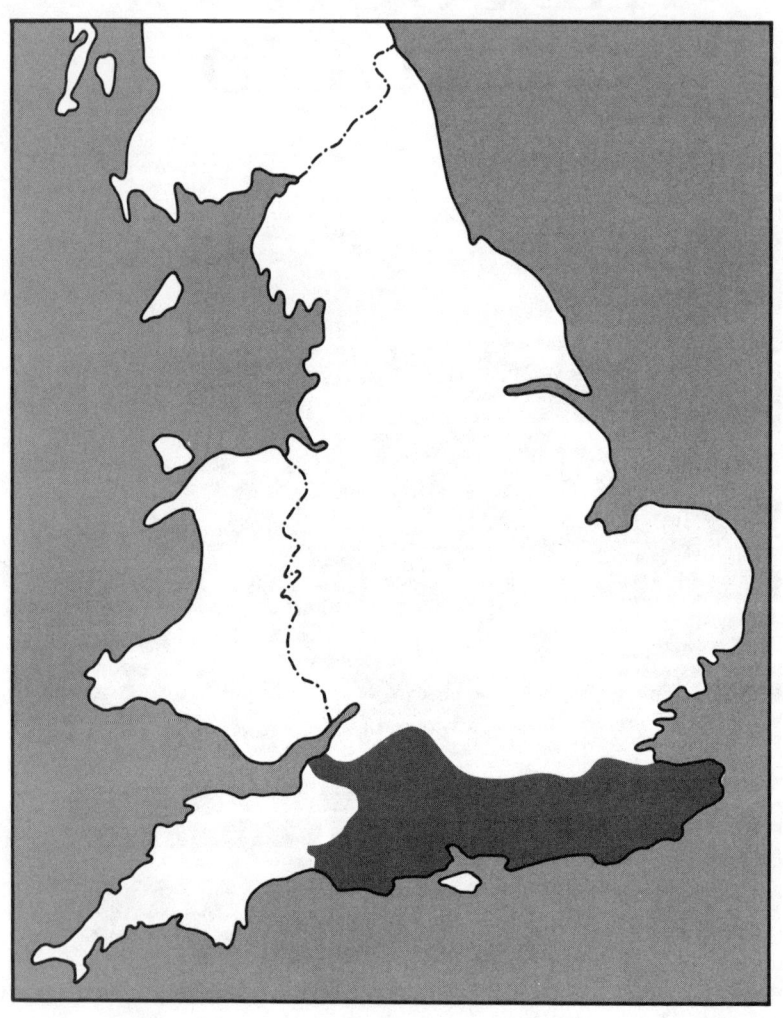

It often occurs to me what an excellent idea it is for each state to have its own little slogan printed underneath each car license plate: "First in Flight," "The Constitution State," and so on. Well, the south of England would represent "The Garden State," like New Jersey. Kent, one of the counties comprising the south of England, is in fact known as the garden of England.

Other counties I include in this area are Sussex, Dorset, and Hampshire. The area is lush, often flat, and has undulating hill ranges that stop rather abruptly at the coastline of the English Channel.

Dorset gets the most sun of all our counties, which is evident when you look at the nice tans and pleasant expressions the locals seem to have. If you visited you'd also notice that the vegetation is almost tropical.

The steep chalk cliffs run a good way along the southern coastline, and on a clear day you can easily pick out the French coast. The English Channel is one of the most congested waterways in the world. It's also one of the most dangerous — rough heavy seas, strong currents, unexpected shallows play havoc with commercial and private shipping.

When you visit the south you'll find much home produce being sold by the roadsides. The main commercial crops are hops (for beer), wheat, barley, many different fruit trees, and, in the last twenty years, grapes. These English vineyards are beginning to make a name for themselves, though many of the vines are still young and produce a rather unsophisticated wine in comparison to their German or French competitors.

It has become the custom for many "east-enders," (those living in the east end of London) to have a working family holiday picking hops in Kent, and year after year the same families will go to the same farm and help gather the harvest—have a break from their everyday job, and get paid in the bargain. My experience is that picking anything for more than a couple of hours is very hard work indeed and you wouldn't get me within a hundred miles of any hop-picking activity.

BAKED EGGS

4 servings
Preparation time: 45 minutes

The English have a lot of different ways of eating eggs, and this is one we do a lot, especially in winter, that's definitely simple, country, English food. You can't make baked eggs unless you have those nice little white, ovenproof ramekin dishes. They look like very small soufflé dishes and have little vertical lines running down the outside. I sometimes make these eggs when I've forgotten to make an appetizer, for I always have eggs in stock. I make one per person if serving them as a starter but as an entrée I can eat three or four, and when you've tried one I expect you will, too.

Special equipment needed: 1 ramekin dish per person, a roasting pan with sides, sharp 4-inch *(10-centimeter)* knife, wax paper

1 *(3/4)* teaspoon lightly salted butter
1 *(3/4)* teaspoon chopped chives
1 sprig of parsley, very finely chopped
Extra butter for greasing
1 large, fresh egg at room temperature

METHOD: Preheat the oven to 300° F. *(150°C.)*. Into your roasting pan put about 1½ inches *(4 centimeters)* of water from the hot tap so that you have made a "bain-marie" (a hot water bath). Place one ramekin dish per person into the tin and put in the oven for 5 minutes. While the dish is warming chop the chives and parsley.
  After the 5 minutes remove the roasting pan from the oven and put the teaspoon of butter into each dish. Allow the butter to melt so that a thin film of melted butter coats the whole inside of the dish; if all the butter doesn't melt that doesn't matter. Then carefully break an egg into each dish and sprinkle the chopped parsley and chives on the top. Cover the surface with a piece of

buttered wax paper to stop the egg's surface from drying out too much.

Return to the oven and gently cook until the yolk is becoming firm but not as hard as a bullet (the white should be firm)—about 40 minutes. Serve hot.

ROAST OF CHICKEN
with Bread Sauce

4 servings
Preparation and cooking time: 2½ hours

You're probably wondering why I'm including a roast of chicken in a book on English cooking. We do it differently and serve it with different accompaniments. I've had so many compliments from Americans on my roast chicken dinners that I feel it is a must. The main difference is in the sauce we serve with chicken—a bread sauce that's absolutely delicious and an ideal taste to accompany chicken. The sauce has been nicknamed "sludge" in our house, and when you make it you'll see why. Americans poke at it very suspiciously the first time, but I notice it's always gone at the end of the meal. We tend to serve bread sauce in preference to cranberry, though we do serve that too.

No English roast would be complete without proper crisp roast potatoes, and I find people rarely serve them in the United States because they require a little effort—not much, mind you. In England a true test of culinary skill might hinge on one's ability to produce a good roast potato—and quite right, too. Learn to follow these instructions and you'll always be able to serve an acceptable meal to anyone—most people eat chicken.

Special equipment needed: a good roasting pan 12 inches by 8 inches *(30 centimeters by 20 centimeters)* or larger with a trivet, a 4-

The South of England 99

quart heavy-bottomed pan, a suction baster, a pair of tongs, open glass, ovenproof casserole dish 12 inches by 8 inches *(30 centimeters by 20 centimeters)*, a 2-quart heavy-bottomed saucepan with lid, a sharp 6-inch *(15-centimeter)* carving knife and fork, a sharp 4-inch *(10-centimeter)* knife, a wooden chopping board, a gravy boat, a large oval serving platter, two wooden spoons (one large and one small), a glass measuring pitcher, a serving bowl for the bread sauce, aluminum foil, a sieve, an oven timer, oven mitts, potato peeler

A 3- to 4-pound *(1350- to 1800-gram)* fresh roasting chicken, with giblets
1 lemon
6 rashers (slices) of bacon
4 small sweet breakfast sausages
BREAD SAUCE
2 cups *(16 fluid ounces)* milk
4 thick slices fresh or stale white bread, with crusts
1 small onion, peeled
10 whole cloves
1 *(3/4)* tablespoon butter
POTATOES
2 pounds *(900 grams)* good, firm potatoes, peeled
1/4 teaspoon *(pinch)* salt
2 cups *(16 fluid ounces)* high-quality corn oil
GRAVY
1 small onion, peeled and roughly chopped
1 bay leaf
3 tablespoons *(3/4 ounce)* unbleached flour
2 cups *(16 fluid ounces)* chicken stock or 2 cups *(16 fluid ounces)* hot water and a chicken bouillon cube
Salt and freshly milled pepper

METHOD: Timing is the most important and the most difficult thing in a meal of this nature—there seems so much to do. It's easy if you follow these steps.
 Preheat the oven to 375°F. *(190°C.)*. The chicken will take the

longest time, so that must go in first and the other things can be done while it's cooking. The conventional time rule for cooking poultry is 20 minutes per pound, but quite honestly I find I always need to cook it longer. Prepare the chicken for the oven by removing the giblets (usually contained in a plastic bag inside the bird) and thoroughly rinse the bird in cold water. Chop the lemon into quarters and tuck them inside the bird, where you found the giblets. Place on a trivet (a trivet will raise the bird off the base of the pan, allowing the heat to reach all around, and will stop the bird from stewing in its own juice—horrid) in the pan, upside down. By this I mean breast side down. This is a trick I've learned when cooking poultry—the juices run through the breast meat, making it white and delicious (thank you, Dorothy Hindley). Now place 2 rashers of bacon over the bird and place on a high shelf in the oven. Set your timer for one hour.

Next prepare the bread sauce. Into a 2-quart heavy-bottomed pan, place the milk and the roughly broken up pieces of bread (no need to remove the crusts). Keeping the onion whole, push the whole cloves into the circumference so it looks like a sputnik, and place that in the bread and milk so that, if possible, it is immersed. Cover with the lid and leave in a warm place, like on the top of the stove. As you know, milk takes on the flavor of other strong smells such as onion, so leave the onion like this for one hour.

Now place the potatoes in a heavy-bottomed 4-quart pan, cover with cold water and a little salt, and quickly bring to the boil. As this is happening, put the corn oil in the glass ovenproof dish. As soon as the potatoes come to the boil, drain them thoroughly and place them in the oil. (I use my suction baster to make sure that oil covers each and every potato.) Set the dish in the oven, on the same shelf as the bird, if possible.

Soon the timer will be going off. Take your little sausages and wrap a rasher of bacon (you have 4 slices left) around each. When the timer sounds remove the bird from the oven and turn it over. Baste well, remove the rashers of bacon on the bird and discard them, place the sausage/bacon accompaniments around the bird in the baking tin, and return it to the oven. Set the timer for 30 minutes.

When the potatoes have been cooking for half an hour, drain off the oil and return them to the oven (briefly baste again). Tidy the kitchen now, wash and put away what you can, or the place will start looking like a national disaster area.

Now you must keep a careful eye on your oven. The bird is coming to the end of its cooking period, and the potatoes should be starting to brown and crisp up—the aim is to have the bird ready a little ahead of the potatoes. Toward the end of the cooking I also remove the lemon to assist the final browning; it will have done its job by now. (You'll need to use tongs so you won't be burned.) The occasional basting helps to brown the chicken, but not much, as most chickens produce quite a lot of fat and manage to baste themselves.

Anyone hanging around the kitchen at this point has to be evicted.

When you are satisfied that the chicken is nicely brown all over, remove from the oven. Final tests for doneness are, first, smell (does it smell cooked?) and, second, carefully push a small knife into the thigh area as deep as you can and check that the juice shows no trace of pink. Remove the chicken and the sausages from the pan and place on a wooden board to rest.

If you are preparing a green vegetable like cabbage or broccoli, do it now.

Remove the onion from the bread sauce, stir with a small wooden spoon, then place over low heat, add the butter, and stir occasionally.

Now make the gravy. Take the pan the chicken has been cooking in, remove the trivet, and then remove and discard about half of the grease. Be careful to extract only the pure grease and none of the browned bits; they're the tasty part. I do this using my suction baster. Using an oven mitt to hold the pan, place it on the stove top over low heat, add the chopped onion and bay leaf, and cook for 5 minutes, stirring occasionally. Sprinkle on the flour and don't worry about lumps forming; it's going to be sieved. Try and let some of the flour in the pan burn a little; this will help to color the gravy. Then introduce the stock a little at a time, stirring all the time and all over the pan, moving the contents over the heat until the consistency that you like is reached. The more stock you add the thinner will be the gravy. Season to taste and pour through a sieve into a gravy boat.

By now the potatoes will be done, so turn off the oven (it will stay hot for ages) but leave the potatoes in. Put the gravy in the oven (cover it with a saucer to stop a skin forming). Now carve the bird. Slice the white meat, then remove the wings and legs in portions. When you have removed as much flesh as possible, save the carcass for making stock and place the meat and sausages on a large oval platter. Arrange the potatoes around the edge. Cover the platter with foil and place in the oven.

Finally check the bread sauce. Stir well but don't scrape the bottom, in case it burned a little. The bread should be completely integrated with the milk and be the consistency of oatmeal. Put in a serving dish and cover with foil.

The green vegetable will keep fresh and hot if you place it in a covered vegetable dish, preferably china.

Now clean up, have a drink, and relax. The meal will keep fresh for at least 20 minutes. Summon the troops when you are ready.

CAULIFLOWER, CHEESE, AND BACON

4 servings
Preparation time: 45 minutes

This is an old family favorite and very popular in English homes, especially when the housekeeping money is getting a little on the low side. Quite apart from cost, this is a scrumptious meal, easy to make, satisfying, and full of good, balanced nutrition. Make sure you choose a nice fresh cauliflower—one that has white, healthy-looking florets.

The South of England

Special equipment needed: a large heavy-bottomed 4-quart saucepan with lid, a 2-quart, heavy-bottomed saucepan with lid, a heavy-bottomed skillet, wooden spoon, tongs, oval serving platter, cheese grater, sharp 4-inch *(10-centimeter)* knife, slotted spoon

1 large fresh cauliflower
2 quarts *(2 liters)* water
¼ teaspoon *(small pinch)* salt
12 lean rashers (slices) bacon
4 tablespoons *(2 ounces, half a stick)* butter
3 level tablespoons *(¾ ounce)* all-purpose flour
1 cup *(8 fluid ounces)* fresh milk
¾ cup *(a bit over 2 ounces)* — or more, if you like cheese — grated sharp Cheddar cheese
1 *(¾)* teaspoon dry English mustard powder
Salt and freshly milled black pepper

METHOD: Timing is important, so follow carefully. Start the meal about 45 minutes before you want to eat. First prepare the cauliflower. Discard some of the more motheaten leaves, then more carefully remove the others and save. Break the cauliflower up into florets — a floret is usually a convenient bite-sized portion. I usually remove the thick stalk and save it. Thoroughly wash everything, making sure you remove all particles of dirt. Next bring about 2 quarts of water to the boil in a heavy-bottomed 4-quart saucepan and add ¼ teaspoon *(pinch)* of salt. When the water boils, throw in the cauliflower, leaves and all, and cover with a lid. You'll probably be able to turn down the heat when it returns to the boil and still keep the vegetable at the boiling point.

In a heavy-bottomed skillet start cooking the bacon on a low flame. Meanwhile, do the cheese sauce. Melt the butter over a medium heat in a 2-quart heavy-bottomed saucepan. Add all the flour and cook for one minute; then pour in all the milk. Stir with a wooden spoon. As the milk heats it will integrate with the butter/flour mixture. The mixture is going to be rather thick; that's okay. It will seem as if the lumps will never go. Keep stirring till they do (use a balloon whisk if you want to hurry it up), then add the grated cheese and mustard, cover with a tight-fitting lid, and put to one side.

Now check the cauliflower, it usually takes 10 to 15 minutes. The stems need to be nearly soft (poke a knife into them to test) — there's nothing more horrible than overcooked cauliflower, so watch it carefully. When it's cooked, strain off the water but save it. Check the bacon; all the rashers must be crisp. Be careful; I'm always burning bacon.

Now take some of the water you cooked the cauliflower in and add to the sauce a little at a time until you get a thick creamy consistency. I do this because the liquid is full of nutrition and that's what's good for you! Check the seasoning. Use plenty of freshly milled black pepper.

Finally, assemble the dish by placing the cauliflower on an oval platter and pouring the sauce over it. Then lay the cooked rashers of bacon over the top as a garnish, and there you have it — very English.

ENGLISH FISH CASSEROLE

6 good servings
Preparation time: 1 hour and 30 minutes

Every American who tastes English Fish Casserole raves about it, and so will you. The nice thing about it — you can make it ahead of time, like the day before, and reheat it, so it's ideal for a dinner party when old friends are coming, because it's no fun if you have to keep your head buried in the kitchen missing all the gossip.

Special equipment needed: a 4-quart heavy-bottomed saucepan with lid, a large, heavy-bottomed skillet with lid, a 2-quart heavy-bottomed saucepan with lid, a slotted spoon, a masher, a sharp 4-inch *(10-centimeter)* knife, a wooden chopping board, an ovenproof glass casserole dish measuring 12 inches by 8 inches *(30 centimeters by 20 centimeters)* with 3-inch *(8-centimeter)* sides, wax paper, a potato peeler, a large pastry bag with large star-shaped tube or a regular fork, a wooden spoon, oven mitts, a juice extractor

2 pounds *(900 grams)* cod fillets (or your favorite soft white fish)
1¼ cups *(8 ounces)* bay scallops (optional)
1 fresh, juicy lemon
Parsley sprigs
⅓ cup *(about 2½ fluid ounces)* medium-dry white wine, preferably the one you're serving at the table
1 medium onion, peeled and diced
TOPPING
4 pounds *(1800 grams)* good firm potatoes
1¼ *(1)* teaspoons salt
2 to 3 tablespoons *(1 to 1½ ounces)* butter or margarine
Salt and a lot of freshly milled pepper
½ cup *(4 fluid ounces)* fresh milk
SAUCE
4 tablespoons *(2 ounces, half a stick)* butter
3 level tablespoons *(¾ ounce)* all-purpose flour
½ cup *(4 fluid ounces)* milk
3 *(2¼)* tablespoons finely chopped parsley
Juice of half a lemon
Salt and freshly milled white pepper

METHOD: There are three stages to this dish and it will take you about an hour and a half to complete the whole thing (don't worry, you'll be able to make a few phone calls in between). So let's go—by dealing with the fish, and scallops if you have them. Wash thoroughly under cold water, then place in a large heavy-bottomed skillet (one that has a lid and is large enough so you can place the fish so no overlapping occurs) with a lemon, quartered, and a few parsley sprigs. Add the wine and enough cold water so the fish is completely covered and place on medium heat. When it comes to the boil, reduce to a simmer, and cover with a lid. If you don't have a lid use a piece of wax paper or a large plate. It will take 10 minutes for the fish to cook; after that put it to one side till you're ready for it.

While this is going on tackle the potatoes. Peel and "eye" them (that means remove the specks that you sometimes get) and cut them into equal small sizes—the smaller you chop them, the quicker they'll cook. Place in a 4-quart heavy-bottomed pan, add ¼ teaspoon *(small pinch)* of salt, cover with cold water, and bring to the boil quickly. When they boil, cover with a lid and simmer till you can easily stick a small knife in them (usually 15 minutes from boiling). When cooked drain all the water and put to one side so that the moisture evaporates.

While the spuds are cooking start the sauce, not a difficult thing to do. In a heavy-bottomed 2-quart saucepan, melt the butter over a medium heat, then add the flour and cook it for 1 minute, then add the milk at one go. Stir with a wooden spoon till the lumps go—don't worry, they will eventually! It will be too thick, so "let it down" (that's a chef's expression for adding liquid) with some of the liquid you cooked the fish in. It needs to be the consistency of slightly whipped cream or melting ice cream. Now add the finely chopped parsley and the lemon juice. Check out the seasoning and add salt and freshly ground pepper to your taste. Put to one side and cover with a lid.

By now the potatoes will have stopped steaming and most of the moisture will have disappeared, so mash them up with a masher and add the butter, remaining teaspoon of salt, and plenty of freshly ground black pepper (don't skimp on the pepper, it needs lots—at least 20 turns). Add the milk, a little at a time, until it's like stiff whipped cream. Don't let it get too sloppy because you've added too much milk.

Finally, assemble the dish by placing the cooked fish in the bottom of a glass ovenproof casserole dish (a slotted spoon will help). It will probably break up as you're doing this; it doesn't matter at all. Now add the diced raw onion, and then pour on the sauce. The last thing is to put the mashed potato on the top. I like to do this with a pastry bag (using my largest star-shaped tube), but if you haven't got one or have hysterics every time you try to use one, just spoon it carefully over the fish and then make pretty crisscross patterns with a fork.

At this stage you can leave to cool *completely* (this is important) before you store in the refrigerator for no more than 24 hours. To reheat, place in a preheated 350°F. *(180°C.)* oven for 30 minutes, then brown the potato topping under the broiler for 5 minutes.

A final word of warning. When you take the hot dish out of the oven and/or broiler *have a care* and use good oven mitts. On several occasions I've dropped the whole thing on the floor and had to serve baked beans instead.

CHOCOLATE ROLL MOUSSE

6 servings
Preparation time: 40 minutes
Cooking time: 20 minutes
Waiting time: 4 hours

Quite honestly this is the most sinful dessert I know, and I make it when I want to impress. It looks great, and tastes so lovely you wonder why you don't make it every day. I once heard a similar dessert described by the head waiter at the River Café in Brooklyn as "a little piece of heaven."

Do not make it for guests the first time (that goes for all recipes you've never cooked before). You'll need to make this dish a few times before you master it, even with my instructions—but even the failures will be devoured rapidly by the family.

This kind of dessert has become popular in England only in the last twenty years, since the middle and upper classes of England have upgraded their kitchens and come to terms with doing household chores themselves. In some upper-class homes an apology for a forthcoming bad meal was phrased: "Cook's night out; sorry!"

Special equipment needed: Pastry brush, wax paper, a 4-inch sharp knife, small, medium, and large stainless steel bowls, 2-quart saucepan (or double boiler), 1 large balloon whisk or hand electric mixer, small wooden spoon, 1 baking tray (16 × 16), 1 large oval serving dish, clean tea towel, a small sieve.

Corn oil for greasing
1 cup *(6 ounces)* bittersweet cooking chocolate or chocolate chips (it *must* be bittersweet)
4 large, fresh eggs at room temperature
¾ cup *(5 ounces)* superfine sugar
2 *(1½)* tablespoons hot water
Butter for greasing
½ pint *(8 fluid ounces)* heavy cream
3 *(2¼)* tablespoons confectioner's sugar

METHOD: Brush a 16-inch by 11-inch *(40-centimeter by 27½-centimeter)* baking tray with oil. (A tray has ½-inch *(1¼-centimeter)* sides, as opposed to a baking sheet, which has just a lip.) Now line the tray with wax paper, letting the sides overlap, and cut a duplicate that you put to one side.

With a small sharp knife cut the chocolate into small pieces and put it in a stainless steel bowl the right size so it will sit snugly over a pan of just simmering water. Leave to melt—that will take about 10 minutes, depending on the atmospheric temperature in your kitchen. While that is going on, separate the eggs. I do this by firmly cracking the shell on a hard surface with a lip and then, over a bowl, I transfer the contents *carefully* from one half shell to another until the white falls away from the yolk. Put the yolks in a medium-sized bowl as you separate them. Add the superfine sugar to the yolks and beat until the mixture becomes thick and light—about 3 minutes. I use a hand electric mixer or a large balloon whisk.

At this point preheat the oven to 375°F. *(190°C.)*. Now add the hot water to the chocolate and stir with a small wooden spoon until all the water is integrated with the chocolate. Then in a large stainless steel mixing bowl whisk the egg whites with a hand electric mixer or balloon whisk (beaters and bowl must be clean) until soft peaks form and you can hold the bowl upside down without the whites falling out.

Now combine everything. With a wooden spoon mix the yolk and sugar mixture with the chocolate, then fold in the beaten egg whites carefully with a balloon whisk. Pour into the prepared baking tray and place on the middle shelf of the oven for 20 minutes exactly.

As it's baking, butter the duplicate piece of wax paper, and when you remove the tray from the oven place this over the top. On top of that put a clean tea towel, which you have run under the cold tap and wrung out beforehand. Now, I'm afraid, you must leave the sheet cake for at least 4 hours, and preferably overnight, at room temperature.

When you are ready to assemble the dessert, whip the cream till stiff (I often find cream won't whip unless it has first been refrigerated). Turn out the cooled chocolate sheet cake onto the buttered wax paper on a working surface, and peel off the greased under paper carefully (it's now on top). Then evenly spread the stiff whipped cream on the chocolate surface.

Now comes the most difficult part of all. You have to roll it. Long end to long end. It will crack as sure as eggs is eggs, but don't worry, persevere! Somehow get it into a roll, then place it *ever so* carefully (sometimes I have to get help with another pair of hands) on a large oval serving dish. Drench in confectioner's sugar by putting the sugar in a sieve and sprinkling repeatedly over the roll. This will make it look pretty and help to cover up the great gaping cracks that always appear when I make it. Refrigerate till coffee time and sit back and receive compliments. As that waiter said, it's out of this world.

BREAD AND BUTTER PUDDING

6 servings
Preparation time: 45 minutes

If you saw this delicious dessert on a menu as Pain au Citron Creme Soufflé you'd order it, wouldn't you? Unfortunately it's called Bread and Butter Pudding, which makes it sound heavy and unappetizing, but it's not, and I don't feel that my poetic license goes far enough to be able to rename an English institution. People line the streets and clamor at my door just to get a whiff when I'm cooking this dessert. By popular demand here's my recipe.

Special equipment needed: a 6-cup round ovenproof soufflé dish, a stainless steel mixing bowl, a balloon whisk, a sharp 4-inch *(10-centimeter)* knife

Butter for greasing
5 slices white bread (stale is okay), crusts removed, thinly spread with butter
½ cup *(about 3 ounces)* raisins
2 pieces lemon rind
2 tablespoons *(1 ounce)* white sugar
3 medium-sized fresh eggs at room temperature
2 cups *(16 fluid ounces)* milk
1 *(¾)* tablespoon brown sugar
GARNISH
½ pint *(8 fluid ounces)* lightly whipped heavy cream

METHOD: Thoroughly grease the soufflé dish (I use a discarded butter wrapping). Butter each slice of bread. Lay a slice of bread, butter side up, in the base of the dish, sprinkle on a few of the raisins, and repeat till bread and raisins are used up, reserving enough raisins to sprinkle on the top. Slide the two pieces of lemon rind down into the dish on opposite sides from each other.

Next place the white sugar in a mixing bowl, break in the eggs, and beat for one minute with a balloon whisk or hand electric mixer. Then add the milk and mix well. Pour this over the bread and push the bread down so it gets soaked, then sprinkle the brown sugar on the top.

Preheat the oven to 425°F. *(220°C.)* and after 5 minutes of preheating place the pudding in. Bake for 30 minutes until the dessert has risen well, the top is crusty and golden brown, and the smell tells you you can't wait any longer.

Serve *immediately* with whipped heavy cream.

GINGERNUT BISCUITS

Makes about 16
Preparation time: 30 minutes

Nothing in this world beats homemade cookies. The credit for inventing them must, I believe, go to the French. The rough translation of the word biscuit is "twice baked," so where do you Americans get "cookies"? It goes back to times when the French bread that wasn't sold would be chopped up, placed back in the oven to dry out completely, and then sold cheap, as a kind of rusk. When we were children (and *always* hungry) my Mom used to chop up stale bread, place it in the oven over very low heat to dry out, then leave the crusty bits lying around—they'd always disappear.

Ginger is a very popular taste in the U.S., so I think ginger cookies will be a great hit. In England you can buy them in most supermarkets but they're *so* much better if you make them yourself . . . and cheaper. This is also a good recipe to make with children—if you supervise them properly.

Special equipment needed: a large mixing bowl, a wooden spoon, a large baking sheet, a wire cooling rack, a spatula, an airtight container (for storage)

1 cup *(5 ounces)* unbleached flour
1¼ teaspoons *(just under 1)* freshly ground ginger
1 *(¾)* teaspoon baking soda
3 tablespoons *(1½ ounces)* white sugar
3 tablespoons *(1½ ounces)* margarine
2 *(1½)* tablespoons Vermont maple syrup (see note)

METHOD: Preheat the oven to 375° F. *(190°C.)*.

Sift the flour, ginger, and baking soda into a large mixing bowl, toss in the sugar, then lightly rub in the margarine with your fingertips till the mixture is crumbly. Add the syrup and mix the lot together to form a stiff paste.

Now divide into sixteen equal pieces. Do this by first cutting the mixture in half, then each half into halves and so on. Be careful; professional cooks always make sure that each cookie is the same size and so must you! Divide accurately.

Now take each piece and roll into a ball between the palms of your hands. Then on a large, lightly greased (use some margarine) baking sheet place each ball, leaving plenty of room for each to expand. Then, using a wooden spoon, press down on each one to flatten it slightly. Pop in the oven and bake for 10 to 15 minutes till your nose tells you they're ready. Remove from the oven and leave on the sheet for a little while. Then, using a spatula, place each on a wire rack for final cooling.

Eat immediately with vanilla ice cream or store in an air-tight container and take on a picnic.

Note: In England we use golden syrup. If you can get it from your specialty store, all the better.

IRISH COFFEE

4 servings
Preparation time: 10 minutes

Irish coffee in an English cookbook? The author's gone mad. (Your worst suspicions are confirmed.) But the truth is that Irish or Gaelic coffee is widely served in restaurants and homes throughout England. It is considered something rather special, for high days or holidays only. Anyone can make it so long as the rules are followed; you mustn't leave out any ingredient. An Irish coffee is one in which good fresh coffee is mixed with Irish whiskey and sugar, and then heavy whipped cream is floated on the top. You *must* have the sugar and the whiskey or the specific gravity of the liquid won't be high enough to support the gobs of cream you float on top. The idea is to sip the hot coffee/whiskey mixture through the cream in such a way that each person gets a mustache of cream round his lips as he drinks.

Special equipment needed: 4 very clean stem wine glasses warmed slightly, a medium-sized stainless steel mixing bowl, a hand electric mixer or balloon whisk, a teaspoon

4 teaspoons light brown sugar
½ cup *(4 fluid ounces)* **Irish whiskey (I use Jamison or Paddy's)**
3½ cups *(28 fluid ounces)* **coffee, freshly brewed and hot (I use a strong after-dinner blend)**
½ pint *(8 fluid ounces)* **heavy cream, chilled and slightly whipped to pouring consistency (you'll have some over for seconds)**

METHOD: In each glass place a teaspoon of sugar and then stir in, with the same spoon, 2 tablespoons *(1 fluid ounce)* of whiskey. Now stir in the coffee, leaving ½ inch *(1¼ centimeter)* clear at the top. Stir each glassful so that the sugar gets well and truly dissolved.

Now position the cup (as opposed to the back) of the spoon so that it is sitting just below the surface of the coffee mixture. Pour on the cream so that the flow hits the spoon. The spoon will help to disperse the cream so that ½ inch *(1¼ centimeters)* of cream will rest on the top. Serve immediately and await your second orders.

Note: If the cream doesn't float it's because you've omitted one of the above steps, or one of your guests doesn't want sugar or whiskey. "Tough," you tell them — an Irish coffee cannot be made without sugar or whiskey.

THE WEST COUNTRY

PUBLISHED WITH KIND PERMISSION OF THE BRITISH TOURIST AUTHORITY.

Don't be fooled by this picture of Bedruthan Steps, North Cornwall. The beach and rocks are huge. The spring tides go in and out so quickly that it's quite possible to get cut off altogether. Then you have to wait eight hours before you can climb back up the steps.

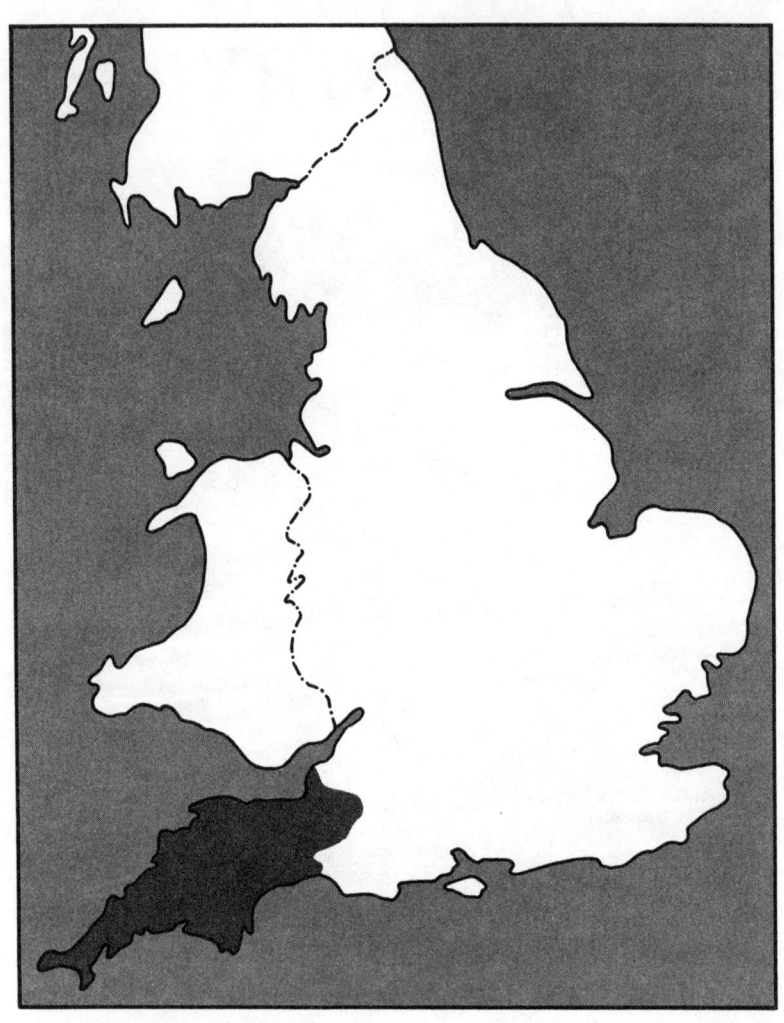

WHEN the English refer to the West Country, they mean Somerset, Devon, and Cornwall. These counties are largely rural. Each county is run in a similar way to a state so that when you're driving along and you cross the county line the surface of the road changes. Yet the difference in counties isn't as large as in states, and if you're being hotly pursued by the police for speeding don't expect them to call a halt as you cross the county line.

Somerset is made up of several low hill ranges with flat pasture land between. It's the home of apple-growing and cider-making. The local cider is called "scrumpy," and unlike American cider is very alcoholic. The leading names are Coates and Woodpecker and they generally make a fizzy cider, which is distributed all over Britain. In Somerset you'll be able to buy flat cider from the wood. This means that it's stored and served from a wooden casket, often in front of you as you order. Watch it if you decide to drink scrumpy—half a pint and you'll be anybody's. I've never seen English cider for sale in America, so if you visit the area you should definitely make a point of sampling a glass.

Devon, on the other hand, is more hilly; lovely undulating hills. If you get good weather this is a really beautiful area to drive through. You should definitely leave the motorway and venture down some of the small roads until you get lost. As in most rural areas of England you'll find the country people very friendly, especially when they discover you're American.

Cornwall and Devon are very popular areas for English "holiday-makers," and you'll encounter a good number of caravans (trailers) on the road. I, too, am very fond of both these areas but if I had to pick one I'd go for Cornwall, the furthest county west. For the romantic, Cornwall has everything. The coastline is often likened to the United States West Coast. Very dramatic cliffs and beautiful stretches of golden sands that get washed twice daily by strong tides. You will find interesting inlets and often rough tempestuous waves indicating heavy seas somewhere in the Atlantic. The whole area is steeped in mysticism, folklore, and stories. Tintagel is one of the most dramatic places you'll visit. It is thought that King Arthur and his Knights of the Round Table headquartered in the castle, the remains of which are precariously perched on top of steep cliffs.

A little further down the coastline is a small fishing village called Port Issac. The houses are old and the whole village is built on a hill, and as each dwelling had a different builder the higgledy-piggledy effect makes the little hamlet look as if it's going to tumble into the cove at the bottom. The roads were built only for horse-drawn vehicles and are too narrow for cars, so you have to park at the top and venture into this wonderful little village on foot and see what excitements are in store for you. If you were with me we'd head straight for the Golden Lion in Fore Street. Some of the window seats in the lounge bar overlook the cove, a sheer drop beneath the window. In winter this pub is the cosiest I know, and you can also get an excellent pint of real ale.

If there is any romance in you at all, an excursion to Bedruthan Steps, still further down the coast, is a must. This is my most favorite beach ever, and because there are over a hundred steps to go down (and up) you usually have large areas of the beach to yourself. There is a very strong, dramatic tide here, and you have to be careful to time your visit in such a way that you hit the sands as the tide is starting to go out or you'll find no beach to run along, or worse, get completely cut off and have to wait another eight hours before you can move. The purchase of a local tide table is a wise investment.

This dramatic and violent tide has the advantage of keeping the whole coastline wonderfully clean. The surfing can be excellent, but dangerous. Each beach has several fatal casualties each year in spite of well-displayed warnings and full-time lifeguards, so please have a care! Bedruthan Steps will give you a huge appetite, and if you have the energy I suggest you arrive early in the day and cook a breakfast of thick English bacon and eggs and brew fresh coffee. There's always tons of driftwood, and a beach fire is just what you'll need after you've been in that cold Atlantic swell for any length of time—the water temperature rarely goes above 60°F.

COCK-A-LEEKIE SOUP

4 to 6 servings
Preparation time: 30 minutes
Cooking time: 2 hours and 15 minutes

The name of this English soup sounds Scottish (and rather rude) when you say it out loud, but its origins are more likely from the West Country. Both of the main ingredients, chicken and leeks, are popular staples in England and readily available here in the States. In England a lunch of soup and cheese is quite normal, and you'll find this particular soup almost a meal in itself.

As with most soups, you can be adventurous and add any tired-looking vegetables that you have; the only thing you have to bear in mind is the cooking time of these additions and add them at the appropriate moment. To make nearly all soups you need to allow one important ingredient, *time*. The basic ingredient of most soups is a good stock — liquor obtained from boiling water with meat, bones, and vegetables. It's the kind of project you do on the side while cooking dinner the night before.

Special equipment needed: a 4-quart heavy-bottomed saucepan with a tight-fitting lid, a colander, a sharp knife, wooden chopping board, a ladle, 2 slotted spoons, a large mixing bowl

1 small chicken or boiling fowl, with giblets
1 medium onion, peeled and roughly chopped
2 medium carrots, peeled and roughly chopped
Bouquet garni (see note)
8 black peppercorns
¼ *(pinch)* teaspoon salt (optional)
8 cups *(64 fluid ounces)* water
6 small or 3 large leeks
¼ cup *(2 ounces)* butter
2 spring onions (scallions), trimmed, washed, and sliced
Salt and freshly milled black pepper
2 *(1½)* tablespoons very finely chopped fresh parsley

METHOD: Thoroughly wash all parts of the chicken, not forgetting to remove the giblets. (You should *always* wash white meat and fish very carefully in lots of cold, running water.) Place the bird whole into your pan and add the onion, carrots, bouquet garni, peppercorns, salt, and water. Bring to the boil quickly, then turn the heat down and simmer for 90 minutes. (You will only need to cook for 30 minutes at the high pressure setting if you want to use a pressure cooker.) From time to time skim off the scum and fat that rises to the surface (I use a ladle for this). If you use a pressure cooker, then skim after cooking.

When the cooking time is up, carefully remove the chicken with two strong utensils (like slotted spoons) and put to one side until it is cool enough to handle. Strain the liquid through a colander into a large bowl, discard the vegetables, and set liquid aside to cool. Place in the refrigerator after the liquid has cooled. Now remove as much of the flesh of the fowl as you can. It's a messy job, most easily achieved with your hands, though you might find a small knife helps. Cut the flesh into small pieces, about ½-inch *(1¼-centimeter)* chunks, but don't waste a lot of time cutting exactly, so long as they are smallish pieces.

When the liquid in the refrigerator has chilled you'll find that the fat has risen to the top and set. How convenient, as we don't want it. Carefully remove it with a slotted spoon and discard.

Now you have an excellent stock. On to the final stage of the soup.

Clean the leeks. This is a job you need to do *very* thoroughly. Dirt manages to get right down inside the leaves (I sometimes wonder how it gets there), and there is nothing worse than encountering grit in a leek when eating. Use lots of cold running water. Trim off the outside leaves and then chop the leeks into small round sections. In a large pan melt the butter, add the leeks and spring onions, cover with a tight-fitting lid, and sweat over medium heat for 5 minutes, shaking to rotate. Then slowly add all your stock, then the chicken pieces. When you are ready to serve, bring slowly to the boil and simmer for 15 minutes, stir well, and add salt and freshly milled pepper to your taste. To serve, sprinkle each portion with a teaspoon of the parsley. This soup will freeze well.

Note: A bouquet garni is a selection of herbs mixed together and put into a small muslin bag. You can buy them, or make your own by mixing half a teaspoon of dried thyme, ground bay leaf, sage, parsley, and rosemary, and tying the ingredients tightly in a piece of muslin.

MY AUNT OCCIE'S GREEN TOMATO CHUTNEY

Makes 10 cups (10 8-ounce jars)
Preparation time: 30 minutes
Cooking time: 70 minutes

Chutney involves the pickling process. Pickling means combining, by cooking, fruits and vegetables with vinegar and sugar so they will preserve — it is a very old method of storage. I presented a similar recipe to *Bon Appetit* magazine, and about three weeks after I had submitted the recipe I had a call from Los Angeles: "Mr. Horan, can you tell me how long will your tomato chutney keep in the refrigerator?"

You don't keep chutney in the fridge. It will keep months in a well-sealed jar in more or less any conditions—that's why it's made. In England it's rather a ritual. The industrious housewife who makes preserves and stocks her freezer with summer fruits also makes a batch of chutney—and jolly good it is too. The habit seems to have died out here, and more is the pity for *it is delicious* and it's not very difficult to make. You eat it with cheese, curries, salads, burgers, hotdogs, and so on. If you make this recipe I guarantee you that your friends will comment on it.

Special equipment needed: 4-quart heavy-bottomed saucepan, wooden spoon, sharp 4-inch *(10-centimeter)* knife, corer, peeler, piece of muslin, 10 8-ounce glass jars with sealed lids

4 pounds *(1800 grams)* green tomatoes
1 pound *(450 grams)* green apples, peeled, cored, and coarsely chopped
1 pound *(450 grams)* onions, peeled and coarsely chopped
1 *(450 grams)* raisins
1 *(3/4)* teaspoon salt
1/2 teaspoon *(large pinch)* ground red pepper
1 *(3/4)* tablespoon English dry mustard
1 1/2-inch *(1 1/4-centimeter)* cube fresh ginger
5 cups *(40 fluid ounces)* cider vinegar (the English would use malt vinegar, but cider's okay)
2 1/4 cups *(1 pound, 450 grams)* light brown sugar dissolved in 1/2 cup *(4 fluid ounces)* more cider vinegar

METHOD: First peel the green tomatoes. This is easily done by taking a small, sharp knife and putting a little cross cut where the tomato would be attached to the plant. Then immerse the whole tomato in very hot water, count to 10, then plunge tomato into cold water; the skin will then easily peel. Chop them coarsely with a small sharp knife and remove as many seeds as you can.

Combine the tomatoes with the apples, onions, raisins, salt, and pepper in a 4-quart heavy-bottomed saucepan. Tie the mustard and ginger in a small piece of muslin and toss that in too.

Pour on enough vinegar to cover and bring quickly to a boil. Add the dissolved sugar/vinegar mixture. Stir well with a wooden spoon. Reduce the heat to a simmer and cook gently for about 70 minutes.

Cool, and then fish out the muslin bag.

You can store in the refrigerator for up to a month or even freeze it, but the best way of keeping it is to bottle. This is very easy to do, so long as you make sure everything is sterile. To sterilize, immerse your containers, tops, and lids in boiling water for 10 minutes; this means that glass containers are best. When properly sterile, fill each jar leaving ½ inch *(1¼ centimeters)* on the top. Cover each surface with wax paper and then seal.

If when you open a jar at a later date, you find a little mold, no matter—scrape it off, discard, and serve the chutney. This is a mold related to the penicillin family and won't do anyone any harm.

PLOUGHMAN'S PLATTER

Preparation time: About 10 minutes

The name "ploughman's platter" is, I think, a recent term invented by British breweries who, wanting to enhance their pubs' menus with local country food, dreamed up the name. It's a rather good name, don't you think? It covers a multitude of different food but usually the main ingredients are bread and cheese. The dish (if one can call it that) is an excellent accompaniment to beer, and that's why you find the best ploughman's platters in pubs.

In writing this "recipe" I'm really planting a seed of an idea in your head rather than giving you specific instructions and quantities (the amounts depend entirely on the number of guests and their degree of hunger). The effort in preparing a decent platter comes in the shopping stage and not in the kitchen. I would never make bread or pâté for this dish—I'd buy it ready-made. However, I would take a little time to search out decent bread and a tasty piece of Stilton, Brie, or Cheddar.

You would choose to make this dish on a day when you would rather be chatting with your friends than worrying what's going on in the kitchen, so it's an ideal meal to serve on a summer weekend for lunch—perhaps outdoors on the lawn or patio.

Special equipment needed: a bread board, sharp bread knife, assorted serving dishes (preferably earthenware), a rustic-looking butter dish

A good hunk of cheese (Cheddar, Brie, Stilton, or your favorite)
A nice crusty loaf (in the United States I usually buy from an Italian bakery)
Butter or margarine
Cherry tomatoes
A bunch of celery, thoroughly washed and divided into stalks
Homemade chutney
Pickled onions
A jar of your favorite mustard (Dijon is good)

METHOD: The wonderful thing about this meal is there's no method. Hurray, you shout. But you do have to set the atmosphere. It's a serve-yourself meal and there's no cooking. So you need to place the bread on an attractive wood chopping board and supply a sharp knife. Arrange the tomatoes in a small basket, put the butter in a butter dish, put the chutney in a pretty earthenware dish, place the celery in a suitable glass pitcher, and provide a plate, knife, and napkin for each person.

I try to use plates with a country, rough-and-tumble look rather than delicate china—after all, I don't think a ploughman breaking for the lunch that his loving wife has traipsed through the fields to bring him would eat from bone china. There's no limit to the foods you can include, so long as the serving of them means little effort for you and the guests can easily help themselves. Do this meal idea, and you'll be eating like hundreds of English families throughout England.

Finally, perhaps you're probably wondering what pickled onions are. They are simply baby onions (shallots) that have been peeled and stored in a sealed jar with a pickling solution consisting largely of vinegar and pickle spices. In England they are readily available in all stores. In the United States you may have to search them out or make them, which is easy enough to do but there's not enough room in this book for a recipe.

CORNISH PASTIES

Makes 10 individual pasties (5 large portions)
Preparation time: 30 minutes
Cooking time: 55 minutes

A Cornish pasty is to the Cornish the equivalent to a slice of pizza, and a great asset as a picnic item. Pasties are attractive looking and you can serve them cold as well as hot. They can be made ahead of time, frozen before cooking, or if cooked will keep in the refrigerator for up to three days. As a meal they would be served with mashed potato, a green vegetable, and a good homemade gravy.

Special equipment needed: a large baking sheet, large mixing bowl, wooden spoon, 5- or 6-inch *(13- or 15-centimeter)* cutter (or any round clean object like a tea plate)

PASTRY

4 cups *(20 ounces)* all-purpose flour
1 cup *(8 ounces)* solid vegetable shortening at room temperature
6 tablespoons *(3 fluid ounces)* ice water
1 *(3/4)* teaspoon salt (optional)
Milk for brushing

FILLING

8 ounces lean ground beef
6 ounces good, firm potatoes, peeled and cut into ½-inch *(1¼-centimeter)* cubes
1 medium sized onion, peeled and diced
1 *(3/4)* teaspoon dried, mixed herbs
Salt (optional) and freshly milled white pepper
4 or 5 tablespoons *(2 to 2⅔ fluid ounces)* beef, chicken, or lamb stock (or gravy)

METHOD: First make the pastry. Combine ½ cup *(2½ ounces)* flour, the shortening, the ice water, and salt in a large mixing bowl and beat with a large wooden spoon. Then, using your fingertips, blend in the remaining flour quickly, without working it too much. You are trying to combine it together and if there isn't enough moisture to do this, then add no more then 3 tablespoons of ice water—not all at once but a little at a time. Gather it into a ball, cover with a damp cloth, and refrigerate.

While the pastry is relaxing mix the beef, potatoes, onion, herbs, salt, and pepper in a bowl and add enough stock or gravy to combine the mixture.

Then divide the pastry, leaving half in the refrigerator. Roll out to about ¹⁄16 inch *(¼ centimeter)* thick and cut 5- or 6-inch *(13- or 15-centimeter)* circles. To do this I use a small tea plate, and try to get 5 rounds. Repeat with the other half of the pastry. Do not reuse the scraps. Instead put them to one side and freeze or refrigerate for another time. (If you use them, you will roll them out twice, and this will cause the pastry to shrink and be tough.)

Preheat the oven to 425°F. *(220°C.)* and lightly grease a baking sheet. Mound meat mixture evenly in the center of each circle and brush each circumference with milk. Fold the pastry over so that one side meets the opposite side and pinch together. The shape should be a half-moon with crinkle edges where you've pinched them together. Brush all over lightly with milk.

Bake for 10 minutes, then reduce the temperature to 325°F. *(160°C.)* and cook for a further 45 minutes until the pastry is a light brown and they smell good.

CHILTON POLDEN PIE

6 servings
Preparation time: 1 hour

Chilton Polden is a small village where my parents now live. It nestles in the Polden hills not far from Glastonbury in Somerset. It is very beautiful, and from my father's garden you can see the moor (a boggy area of marsh land) stretching out for miles. On the other side of the range is Sedgemoor, famous because it was the site in 1685 of the last battle of civil strife in England between James II with 4,000 men and the Earl of Monmouth with 5,000. Monmouth's side was mostly peasants, and they were defeated with heavy losses.

The place is rather sleepy; the occasional dog barks, and there's an excellent general store and a post office. Mrs. Coombes, the postmistress, personally stamps all mail leaving the village, which means she gets to see who is writing to whom. Every letter I receive from home has a little handwritten message from her saying something like "Happy cooking" or "When are you next going to be on TV?"

Gardens in the West Country are worth a mention. People in this area would *never* refer to their gardens as back yards, for in many instances these gardens represent hours of toil and love.

They are open to anyone who wants to peer over the walls and hedges and take a look. If you were to peer over my father's wall from spring to fall you'd see a wonderful splash of color from an array of herbaceous flowers, and a lawn that has been mown in all directions so it has a beautiful crisscross effect. If you were really to stretch you'd be able to see his kitchen garden by the barn. There he grows strawberries, raspberries, black currants, French beans, tomatoes, potatoes, marrows (summer squash), gooseberries, cherry plums (a specialty of Somerset), rhubarb, courgettes (zucchini), and aubergines (eggplant).

This recipe is my invention entirely, and once again don't be put off because it's called a pie. It could just as easily be called a casserole, but then it wouldn't be English, would it? The crust in this instance is the mashed potato topping. The main body of the pie is chicken in a white wine sauce. If you serve a green veggie you'll have a completely nutritious meal.

Special equipment needed: a large heavy-bottomed skillet with 3-inch *(8-centimeter)* sides, a 4-quart heavy-bottomed saucepan, an ovenproof glass oblong casserole dish measuring approximately 8 inches by 12 inches *(20 centimeters and 30 centimeters)* with 2-inch *(5-centimeter)* sides (or larger), a potato peeler, a masher, a large pastry bag with a large star tube (optional) or a fork, a sharp knife, a juice extractor, wooden spoon

4 tablespoons *(2 ounces, half a stick)* butter
1 medium onion, peeled and diced
2 pieces lemon rind
1 bay leaf
3 boneless chicken breasts, roughly cut into 1-inch
   (2½-centimeter) cubes
3 level tablespoons *(¾ ounce)* all-purpose flour
⅓ cup *(about 2½ fluid ounces)* medium-dry white wine
   (preferably the same wine you'll be serving)
Juice of half a lemon (make sure it's a nice, fresh, yellow,
   juicy one)
1 clove garlic, peeled and finely minced
2 cups *(16 fluid ounces)* fresh milk
Salt and freshly milled white pepper
MASHED POTATO TOPPING
3 pounds *(1350 grams)* good-quality, firm potatoes, peeled,
   and left to soak in slightly salted water.
4 tablespoons *(2 ounces, half a stick)* butter or margarine
Salt to taste (optional)
Plenty of freshly milled black pepper (I use at least 20 turns
   of my mill)
⅓ cup *(about 2½ fluid ounces)* fresh milk

METHOD: In a large, heavy-bottomed skillet melt the butter and then add the onion. Cook over a medium heat until translucent, about 5 minutes. Then add the lemon rind, the bay leaf, and the chicken breasts (don't forget to rinse them off in cold water first). Continue to cook over a medium heat for 10 to 15 minutes until the chicken is cooked to a light brown color. Do not let the pan get too hot or the butter will burn and that will give the dish an ugly flavor and color.

Now add the flour and stir well with a wooden spoon. Then, stirring all the time, add the wine and lemon juice and allow to cook for 1 minute. Add the garlic. Then add all but ⅓ cup *(about 2½ fluid ounces)* of the milk all at once and continue to stir till a smooth consistency is reached. If the sauce is a little too thick, add the rest of the milk. You're going to tell me, "It's all lumpy!" My reply is, "Keep stirring till they all go." Season to taste, cover with a tight-fitting lid, and put to one side.

Then deal with the potatoes. Drain them and then "eye" (remove the little black indents that you usually find when a potato is peeled). Chop into approximately 2-inch *(5-centimeter)* cubes; try to cut the pieces so they are the same size or they will cook unevenly. Place in a large, 4-quart saucepan, cover with water, and bring to the boil on a high heat. When the water boils, turn down to a rolling simmer and cook until a knife easily slips through the potatoes—about 15 minutes once they boil.

Thoroughly drain potatoes and leave for 5 minutes to allow the water to evaporate. Then add the butter, salt, and pepper. Now get your arm into action and pulverize with a hand masher. I have tried a number of ways of mashing, including using mixers, processors, and forks, but always come back to my hand masher in the end. Now you have to add the milk until you get a smooth but firm consistency. Add the milk slowly; the amount you need will depend on the potato you are using and the humidity of the kitchen. Do not put so much in that they become sloppy—they should be soft but firm.

Now transfer the chicken and sauce into the glass ovenproof dish. When it is cool enough to handle transfer the potato into a pastry bag with a large star tube and pipe the potato in simple rows over the chicken.

To serve, heat in a 300°F. *(150°C.)* oven for 20 minutes and then brown the potato topping under the broiler for a few minutes.

Note: I've tried a dozen times to write a paragraph on how to use a pastry bag and can't adequately find words that help to describe to a novice how to do it. I've also tried to draw diagrams, but these don't help either. I have spent hours with my students practicing with instant potato and they still don't really seem to get it. Some people just aren't coordinated enough to do it. It's a knack that either comes with experience or doesn't, and there's only one way to learn—trial and error. If you keep doing it you will discover for yourself the best way. For the purposes of this recipe you could just spread the potato with a fork and then make an indented pattern with the tines of a fork.

CREAM TEAS

Preparation time: 20 minutes
Makes about 10

This recipe for scones (rhymes with stones, as the famous writer Zack Hanle reminded me). If anything is going to make you fat, a cream tea is a sure bet. As with a ploughman's platter, the effort in making a cream tea is more setting the atmosphere than anything else. Attention has to be paid to the little things like doilies, pretty pots for the preserves, a special spoon for the preserve, and so on.

As you drive through Devon and Cornwall you'll see a sign at every twist in the road saying "Cream Teas." This is an opportunity for you to gorge yourself, so jam on the breaks as soon as you see a sign by a homestead that appeals to you. You probably won't be able to fit yourself back in your car after. The idea behind a cream tea is to sell cream—a large industry in these parts. Nothing can beat the taste of double Devonshire cream or clotted Cornish cream. When I was a teenager I used to walk to the farm near our holiday home, buy a whole pint of clotted cream (where it was made on the premises) and a jar of best-quality preserves, and sneak back to the kitchen, unnoticed. I'd get a teaspoon out and eat the lot. It's a wonder I never developed a weight problem!

A scone is merely a vehicle for you to be able to get the preserves and cream into your mouth, and the tea is served merely to wash it all down. Everyone here in America thinks scones are so difficult to make. I've news for you; they're so easy a child could make them. But I always produce them in a flourish, and smile sweetly (nodding all the time) when people say, "I wish I could make scones like these." My response is that it takes years to perfect the complicated recipe, so please, let's keep this one between ourselves, yes?

Scones are very similar to what you Americans call biscuits. Biscuits are, on the other hand, something quite different in England. They are cookies, just to confuse you.

Finally, I'm afraid I have to smash another misconception about the English. Today's average Englishman doesn't talk as if he had a plum in his mouth, nor does everything stop for afternoon tea. Tea in England is treated rather as Sunday brunch is here in the United States. It's something one does occasionally, more for fun than anything else. It's true the English drink a lot of tea in the same way as one pauses at work to drink a soda here, but a "proper" tea with cakes, sandwiches, scones, jam, and cream is a thing of the past and only occasionally practiced for special visitors. Here's how to make the scones I serve.

Special equipment needed: a large (preferably china) mixing bowl, a sieve, a 4-inch *(10-centimeter)* knife or a fork, a 1- to 1½-inch *(2½- to 4-centimeter)* crinkled round pastry cutter, a baking sheet, a wire cooling rack, a rolling pin, a pastry bag and large star tube

2 cups *(10 ounces)* all-purpose flour
1⅓ tablespoons *(⅔ ounce)* butter or margarine at room temperature
1½ *(1⅛)* tablespoons superfine sugar
¼ teaspoon *(small pinch)* salt
½ cup *(about 3 ounces)* raisins (optional)
⅔ cup *(about 5 fluid ounces)* fresh milk
Flour for rolling out
GARNISH
½ pint *(8 fluid ounces)* heavy cream

METHOD: Preheat the oven to 425°F. (220°C.). Sift the flour into a large mixing bowl and then rub in the butter, using your fingers, till it resembles coarse meal. Stir in the sugar, salt, and raisins. Then add the milk slowly, stirring with a fork. Use your hands to finish off the mixing process and knead the mixture to a soft dough. If you're in a very dry atmosphere you may need to add a little more milk.

Turn the dough out onto a lightly floured working surface and roll out to about a ¾-inch *(2-centimeter)* thickness with a rolling pin.

Cut the scone shapes using a crinkled pastry cutter. Make firm cuts. When you've cut as many as you can, knead the mixture again and continue to cut till all the mixture is used up. (Sometimes I use a smaller pastry cutter to make smaller scones—the mix goes further and it looks as if you've worked harder than you really have.)

Place scones on a greased baking sheet, leaving a little space between each, and bake for 12 to 15 minutes until golden brown. (Slightly less time if you use a smaller cutter.) Turn out on a wire cooling rack.

To serve I usually slice horizontally in half. The English treat each half as follows: They spread a little butter or margarine onto the surface, then spread on a blob of good strawberry or red raspberry preserves. I usually pipe a good helping of whipped heavy cream on the top using a pastry bag and a large star-shaped tube. You won't be able to get real clotted cream here; heavy cream is the nearest thing, and if you can't pipe it on, then spoon it on. Place each treated half on an oval serving plate on which you've placed a white napkin or doily. Scones don't keep, so eat them while they're hot.

Serve with a pot of freshly brewed loose-leaf tea and make it in a proper china pot (use China, Indian or Ceylon (Sri Lanka) tea. Warm the pot first; then, using fresh water, pour onto the leaves *right at the moment the water boils,* never before—one teaspoon of tea per person and one for the pot is the recognized English rule. Leave the tea to brew for 5 minutes (no longer), then serve with milk or lemon. Filter off the leaves when pouring by using a tea strainer.

There, now—that isn't difficult, is it?

APPLE SNOW

8 servings
Preparation time: 45 minutes
Chilling time: at least 1 hour

Next time you find yourself with yet another gift of apples in the fall, remember this recipe. It turns apples into a cold soufflé like magic, and it's so easy you hardly have to think while you're making it (I'm surprised restaurants don't serve it). The West Country gets the recipe because of all the orchards. As you drive through Somerset and Devon in the fall you can almost smell the apples!

Special equipment needed: a 2-quart heavy-bottomed saucepan with lid, a large stainless steel mixing bowl, a hand electric mixer or a large balloon whisk, 8 stem wine glasses, juice extractor, sharp 4-inch *(10-centimeter)* knife, fine mesh sieve

5 large, tart green apples, peeled, cored, sliced, and left to soak in water and ¼ teaspoon *(small pinch)* salt or the juice of half a lemon
1 *(¾)* level teaspoon cinnamon
3 cloves
2 *(1½)* tablespoons light brown sugar
Juice of half a nice, fresh, yellow lemon
2 pieces lemon rind
3 large, fresh egg whites at room temperature
1 cup *(about 7 ounces)* superfine sugar
½ pint *(8 fluid ounces)* heavy cream, whipped (optional)

METHOD: Put the apples into a large saucepan with no more than 1 cup *(8 fluid ounces)* of water and add the cinnamon, cloves, brown sugar, and lemon juice and rind. Cover the pan and bring to the boil on medium heat, then turn down to a simmer. Apples produce a lot of water in cooking and we want the apples to break down to a pulp without being too watery, so we must use enough water so they don't burn but not enough to make them sloppy when cooked. As they cook, check that they aren't burning and stir them so the apples on the top get some of the heat. They will only take about 10 minutes (if that). When they are tender, drain them thoroughly in a sieve. Remove the lemon peel and cloves, and put aside to cool.

In a metal bowl (stainless steel is good) whisk the egg whites till they form soft peaks (they're ready when you can tip the bowl upside down and they hold firm) — I use a hand mixer. Remember not to overwhisk or you'll beat out the air you've so carefully put in. Then add the sugar, ⅙ of a cup *(1⅛ ounces)* at a time, whisking between each addition.

Gently combine the cooled apples with the meringue mixture and pour into 8 stem serving glasses (I use wine glasses). Refrigerate until ready for service (at least 1 hour). A blob of slightly whipped heavy cream goes well to decorate the top.

PENELOPE PITT'S GINGER BEER

Makes 10 U.S. pints
Time needed: 16 days (don't worry, it's worth it)

When I was a child, my mother would long for us children to announce that we were leaving home for good, which we did daily, and then she could get on with her book. For me it meant getting on my bike and taking off to various long-suffering neighbors' homes to see what was cooking, for I was constantly hungry, even after a meal. Mrs. Pitt's answer to my quest for food was occasionally the offer of a glass of her homemade ginger beer.

She recently gave me the recipe, and seeing as ginger beer is beginning to become popular in the States, I am including it in this section, for most pubs in the West Country will sell it. Make it once by carefully following these instructions and you'll make it for the rest of your life, for it is absolutely delicious. Don't be confused by the term 'plant.' In this instance I use it because you are establishing a chemical reaction as one does in an industrial plant.

Special equipment needed: a wooden spoon, a glass juice jar, a clean 10-quart plastic container, 5 clean plastic or glass 1 litre *(33.8 fluid ounces)* screw-top bottles, a small china or plastic mixing bowl, a piece of muslin, a small funnel, a 4-quart heavy-bottomed saucepan

INGREDIENTS TO MAKE THE PLANT
2 ounces fresh baker's yeast (a good bakery will sell you this)
2 *(1½)* level tablespoons superfine sugar
2 *(1½)* level tablespoons freshly ground dried ginger bought from a spice store and *not* a supermarket
1¼ cups *(10 fluid ounces)* water
INGREDIENTS TO FEED THE PLANT
10 *(7½)* level teaspoons freshly ground dried ginger
10 *(7½)* level teaspoons superfine sugar
INGREDIENTS TO COMPLETE THE PROCESS
19 cups *(152 fluid ounces)* water
2 large fresh lemons
2¼ cups *(15¼ ounces)* superfine sugar

METHOD TO MAKE THE PLANT: Mix the yeast and sugar together in a small, clean plastic or china bowl with a small wooden spoon. You will find that the grittiness of the sugar will help you to break up the yeast so that a paste forms. Add the ginger and slowly mix in ¼ cup *(2 fluid ounces)* of hand-hot water (hand hot is much hotter than you think). Stir till well blended, then add a further cup of hand-hot water and place in a very clean glass jar (I use a discarded glass juice bottle) and leave, uncovered, in a warm place.

METHOD TO FEED THE PLANT: Each day feed the plant. Do this by sprinkling onto the surface 1 *(¾)* teaspoon of superfine sugar and 1 *(¾)* of ginger. Do this for 10 days.

METHOD TO COMPLETE THE PROCESS: When the 10 days are up, take a heavy-bottomed 4-quart pan and dissolve 2¼ cups *(15¼ ounces)* of superfine sugar with 3¾ cups *(30 fluid ounces)* of water. Heat slowly, stirring with a wooden spoon, until the sugar is dissolved; it doesn't take long.

Now take a very large container (I use a thoroughly cleansed 10-quart plastic bucket), and pour in the sugar and water mixture. Then add 2½ cups *(20 fluid ounces)* of cold water and the strained juice of two lemons. Now add 12½ cups *(100 fluid ounces)* of cold water. Take the plant you've been feeding for 10 days and strain the liquid through muslin into the bucket. If you haven't any muslin then you'll have to sacrifice an old, clean, T-shirt. Save the sludge if you want to make more. Stir all the liquid well and pour into screw-top bottles. The new 2½-liter plastic screw-top soda bottles are ideal for this. Fill each bottle, leaving about a 2-inch *(5-centimeter)* air gap at the top for the ginger beer to breathe — I find a small funnel helps. Place the tops on but don't tighten down till the following day.

Sample after 5 days, covering the neck of the bottle with a cloth when opening. A small amount of sediment may collect at the bottom of the bottle. I find the best way to avoid serving this is to carefully, at one go, decant the contents of the bottle into a pitcher, taking care that the sediment remains in the bottle. Serve chilled, and *not* to children, for it is alcoholic. Dilute with a lemonade soda or beer to make a refreshing shandy.

To continue the plant, divide the sludge into two glass juice containers, add 1¼ cups *(10 fluid ounces)* of hand-hot water to each and feed the plant in the previous manner. You'll then be running two plants and will be making double the amount. Cheers!